P9-CKG-848

THE HERB GARDENER

A Guide for All Seasons

Susan McClure

A Storey Publishing Book

**STOREY
BOOKS**
Schoolhouse Road
Pownal, Vermont 05261

The mission of Storey Communications is to serve our customers by publishing practical information that encourages personal independence in harmony with the environment.

Edited by Elizabeth McHale and Gwen Steege
Front cover design by Laurie Musik Wright
Cover photograph by © Jane Grushow and Grant Heilman Photography, Inc.
Text design and production by Greg Imhoff
Color illustrations by Brigita Fuhrmann
Indexed by Northwind Editoral Services

Copyright © 1996 by Susan McClure

All rights reserved. No part of this book may be reproduced without written permission from the publisher, except by a reviewer who may quote brief passages or reproduce illustrations in a review with appropriate credits; nor may any part of this book be reproduced, stored in a retrieval system, or transmitted in any form or by any means — electronic, mechanical, photocopying, recording, or other — without written permission from the publisher.

The information in this book is true and complete to the best of our knowledge. All recommendations are made without guarantee on the part of the author or Storey Books. The author and publisher disclaim any liability in connection with the use of this information. For additional information, please contact Storey Books, Schoolhouse Road, Pownal, Vermont 05261.

Storey Books are available for special premium and promotional uses and for customized editions. For further information, please call Storey's Custom Publishing Department at 1-800-793-9396.

Printed in the United States by R.R. Donnelley and Sons Company
10 9 8 7 6 5 4

Library of Congress Cataloging-in-Publication Data
McClure, Susan 1957–
      The herb gardener : a guide for all seasons / Susan McClure.
          p. cm.
      "A Storey Publishing book."
      Includes bibliographical references (p.) and index.
      ISBN 0-88266-910-9 (hc.: alk. paper). — ISBN 0-88266-873-0 (pbk.: alk. paper)
      1. Herb gardening.   2. Herbs.   I. Title.
SB351.H5M343   1995
635'.7—dc20   95-37999
                                                                  CIP

Contents

© Kevin Kennefick

© Kevin Kennefick

© Kevin Kennefick

PART ONE

About Herbs

CHAPTER 1

WHAT IS AN HERB?

*I*magine jars of dried green tarragon, pesto on steaming pasta, or a neatly kept knot garden. All are herbs in different forms. You can define herbs broadly to include almost any plant, or you can modify the definition to encompass the classic herbs cherished for their fragrance and flavor. If you only have a small space for herb gardening, you might stick with the most useful of the herbs, going by a strict definition. Or if your yard is large and your horizons are broad, you can expand your garden to include herbs with a romantic past, even if you really don't use them much. Let's explore several definitions of herbs and what each means for your herb garden.

An herb is a plant that has fragrance, flavoring, or medicinal value. This definition includes most herbs that are sold commercially, plus all kinds of plants cherished through history or valued today for their aromatic, flavorful, or healing qualities. But a few herbs — plants with everlasting flowers or foliage for crafting, or colors that dye textiles — are missing from this definition.

An herb has soft stems. Botanical textbooks define an herb as any herbaceous, nonwoody plant that dies back to the ground at the end of its growing season. It may be an annual, living just one growing season or until it sets seed, or it may be a biennial or perennial, living two or more growing seasons. But in either case, the stems stay soft. (For more information on life cycles, see Chapter 3.)

This definition of an herb is more appropriate to an herbaceous border of flowers than to a garden of culinary or fragrant herbs. But it is one that explains the presence of a variety of ornamental plants in your herb garden. Yet this definition alone would be too limiting for most herb gardens. It would exclude the many popular herbal shrubs or trees such as sage, rosemary, lavender, rose, thyme, and sweet bay.

~

(Opposite page)

Low-growing thymes provide excellent ground cover in this sunny garden.

~

Photo: © Rosalind Creasy

Plant Names

The Swedish botanist Linnaeus devised a classification system that divided and subdivided the entire plant kingdom. Today we use rules based on the Linnean system, dividing plants into family, genus, species, and cultivar.

Species is the basic unit of classification. Members of a species have many characteristics in common — they can interbreed like animals such as cats. But they differ from related plants in one or more ways.

Genus (pl., genera) is a larger group of related plants with several features in common, similar to the kinds of characteristics that members of your own family share. A genus may contain one or many different species.

Family is an even larger group of related plants that contains one or more genera.

Let's look at some examples: Mint, lavender, and oregano all belong to the family Labiatae, but each of them is in a different genus. Mint, for example, belongs to the genus Mentha. Mentha contains many mint species, two of which are Mentha spicata (spearmint) and Mentha suaveolens (apple mint). Notice that the genus name is capitalized and put first, followed by the species name.

Scientists use two other terms to further classify plants: hybrid and cultivar. A hybrid is a new plant created by the successful cross-pollination of two different plants. Hybrids display some of each parent's traits. A cultivar, on the other hand, is a term used to describe a plant created purposely by breeders or accidentally through hybridization, mutation, or selection, and then perpetuated under cultivation. Mentha spicata 'Variegata' is a cultivar of apple mint with cream-and-green variegated leaves.

Herbs can be found in all the major plant types — including trees, shrubs, herbaceous perennials, annuals, biennials, and vines. Sweet bay *(Laurus nobilis),* for example, is a tree. Hyssop *(Hyssopus officinalis)* is an example of an herb that is a shrub. There are many herbaceous perennials: lady's mantle *(Alchemilla vulgaris),* licorice *(Glycyrrhiza glabra),* fennel *(Foeniculum vulgare),* cardamom *(Elettaria cardamomum)* — to name just a few. There are also many annual herbs: garden basil *(Ocimum basilicum),* dill *(Anethum graveolens),* chervil *(Anthriscus cereifolium),* and calendula *(Calendula officinalis)* are good examples. Biennials — plants that complete their growing cycle in two years, flowering the second year — include angelica *(Angelica archangelica),* caraway *(Carum carvi),* chicory

(Cichorium intybus), and parsley *(Petroselinum crispum)*. Some herbs grow as vines, such as black pepper *(Piper nigrum)*. And some herbs grow as ferns, for example, Maidenhair fern *(Adiantum capillus-veneris)*, or as seaweed, such as bladderwrack *(Fucus vesiculosus)*.

An herb grows in temperate climates. This definition helps explain the difference between herbs and spices. Generally, herbs grow in temperate climates with a cool winter period. Spices, such as cinnamon and nutmeg, grow in warm tropical or subtropical climates — although ginger and cardamom will grow in cool climates in a sunny window or greenhouse. There are also a few plants that we consider spices that can be grown outdoors in temperate climates and are well worth including in your garden. Most of the temperate spices — such as mustard, coriander, and anise — yield aromatic seeds, which sets them apart from herbs grown for foliage.

You can see that herbs are celebrated for many uses — medicinal, culinary, aromatic, crafting, and ornamental. A perfect definition for herbs (or spices) is hard to pin down. For most gardeners, herbs are those plants that earn their way into our gardens by being delicious for cooking, wonderfully fragrant, or adorned with beautiful flowers or fruit pods for making decorations. Whether our interests are in dye plants or historical herbs, our gardens should bring us beauty and enjoyment every day of the year. This is the philosophy around which this book is based.

Let's look at the herbs that we commonly enjoy. If we examine their homelands we can learn what conditions to provide in order for those herbs to flourish in our gardens.

Horseradish

CHAPTER 2

HERBS & THEIR NATIVE HABITATS

What you consider common herbs may be native to your area or may have come from across the sea. You can learn what kind of growing conditions an herb thrives in by considering where it originated. Similarly, you can find the herbs that will be ideally suited to your blend of sun and shade, soil type, temperature range, and average moisture. Such information will give you a sound start for a low-maintenance herb garden.

Well-Drained, Sunny Sites

If you have a sunny site, you can choose from many of the most popular herbs such as thyme, oregano, lavender, fennel, rosemary, and sage. These plants thrive in sun-drenched, sandy soils and arid conditions similar to their homelands in the Mediterranean region. Full sun, minimal rain, and lean soil combine to produce slower-growing plants with intense, concentrated flavors and fragrances. Under more lush conditions, these plants will survive if the soil is well drained, but the growth will be softer and the foliage will be less aromatic.

Moist, Shady Sites

Herbs for shady or moist sites come from wooded and wet areas worldwide. They may grow in shady glens, mature woodlands, or the sheltered banks of streams. Most need a regular supply of moisture — but few grow in waterlogged soil. Some herbs, such as sweet woodruff, require the protection of shade to keep their foliage from burning. Others, such as bee balm and mint, can grow in sun if given a rich, moist soil.

(Opposite page)
Lavenders thrive in the warm, sunny sites similar to their native habitats.

Photo: © Dency Kane

7

Herbs for Well-Drained, Sunny Sites

Herb	Classification	Description	Qualities
English lavender	hardy or tender shrubs	silver, needlelike leaves and fragrant flowers	sweet, perfumed aroma to leaves and flowers
Fennel	hardy perennial	lanky growth pattern	licorice flavored
Rosemary	tender shrub	needlelike leaves with handsome flowers	pungent flavor to foliage
Sage	hardy shrub	silver leaves and pretty clusters of flowers	pungent flavor to foliage
Thyme	woody perennial	low-growing; fine-textured leaves and clusters of small flowers	delightfully aromatic leaves; cultivars of many flavors

© Liz Ball, Photo/Nats

This well-drained, sunny herb garden site is perfectly suited for the dill, curly and opal basils, fennel, and cilantro growing there.

Herbs for Moist, Shady Sites

Herb	Classification	Description	Qualities
Angelica	hardy biennial or perennial	licorice-flavored stems	coarse texture and majestic appearance in garden
Bee balm	hardy perennial	handsome flowers in summer	mild sweet leaves and flowers; flowers attract hummingbirds
Mint	hardy perennial	vigorous-growing ground cover	varied minty aromas to leaves
Parsley	biennial	rich green frilly or flat leaves; needs rich moist soil in full sun or light shade	clean, fresh flavor to leaves
Sweet woodruff	hardy perennial ground cover	sparkling, small, white flowers in spring	when dried, leaves have a fresh, clean fragrance

© Rosalind Creasy

Container-grown garlic chives and lemon balm benefit from afternoon shade as well as the brick floor, which retains moisture and heat.

© Dency Kane

Artemisia and sage thrive in this cool-climate New England herb garden.

Cool Climates

Some herbs thrive in cool temperatures; others actually detest heat. You can grow herbs originally from cool climates in northern climates with cool growing seasons, moderate climates with cool spring and fall weather, or in southern climates during cool and mild winter weather. Cool-climate herbs cannot tolerate high humidity or hot direct sun.

Warm Climates

In climates that are warm all year round or have hot summers, you can enjoy herbs that originated in the world's warmer climes — many are adapted to sticky summer humidity and sullen heat that can wilt northern herbs. But they only last through winter if kept in a protected, frost-free location, indoors or out.

Herbs for Cool Climates

Herb	Classification	Description	Qualities
Arugula	hardy annual	coarse-toothed leaves and tall flowering stem	leaves have pleasant mustard-garlic flavor
Cilantro	hardy annual	divided leaves on upright plant	pungent foliage and sweetly aromatic seeds ("coriander")
Garlic	perennial	tall, blue-green leaves with occasional ball-shaped flowers	healthful garlic-flavored bulbs, greens, and flowers
Mustard	hardy annual	coarse-toothed leaves and tall flowering stem	spicy flavored leaves and seeds
Welsh onions	hardy perennial	clumps of upright onion-like greens	mild onion-like flavor similar to scallions

Herbs for Warm Climates

Herb	Classification	Description	Qualities
Basil	annual	mounded plants with green or purple foliage; grow during warm, frost-free weather	somewhat clove-flavored leaves
Beefsteak plant	annual	mounded plants with green or purple leaves	foliage with spicy, minty leaves
Ginger	tender perennial	tall, linear leaves with flashy flowers	spicy-aromatic rhizomes; bring indoors in winter in cold climates
Mexican mint marigold	tender perennial	small daisylike flowers	foliage with licorice-mint fragrance
Sweet bay	tender tree	glossy, elliptic leaves on small tree	intensely aromatic foliage; bring indoors in winter in cold climates

© Lee Anne White / Positive Images

This formal garden in the South features dwarf boxwood (*Buxus microphylla* 'Kinsville Dwarf').

PART TWO

Herb Gardening Basics

CHAPTER 3

INTRODUCTION TO HERBS

*I*f you want to get the most out of every single herb you plant, get to know how each grows before you assign it a spot in your garden. You'll soon see that some herbs grow quickly and others grow slowly; some give their all in a short life and others live for decades; some thrive in warm weather and others prefer cool weather.

Learn about all of these factors so you can start determining what you want in your garden. You can choose from annual, biennial, and perennial herbs that live one year, two years, or more. The short-lived annuals and biennials give you flexibility; the long-lived perennials offer security and durability.

As you saw in the last chapter you will be most successful if you choose herbs whose native habitat is similar to the climate and other conditions in your garden. Herbs that prefer cool weather are great for cold northern climates — some can endure the worst cold that northern states can dish out. Others can take sultry summer heat or aridity without breaking into a sweat — they're perfect for hot southern weather. If you like an easy-care herb garden, consider your area's average temperatures and choose the plants that are best suited to it. (Specific information on origins and culture of each herb is given in Part Five, beginning on page 177.)

Even if your favorite culinary or fragrant herb just so happens to be a little tender for your area, you may still be able to grow it. You'll find plenty of tips to help you stretch the heat tolerance and cold hardiness of herbs on page 25. But learn where to get replacement plants, just in case you have to weather the loss of your favorite herb.

(Opposite page)
This colorful herb garden features lavender cotton and variegated, common, and pineapple sages, with tall angelica towering behind.

LIFE CYCLES & GARDEN PLANNING

*O*nce you get to know how long different herbs will live — and how long they take to begin to produce foliage, seeds, or roots for your harvest — you'll know just what to expect in the garden. Here are some of the herb life cycles you'll run into and how they influence your garden planning and harvesting.

Annuals. If you have grown bedding plants such as zinnias and marigolds, you will be familiar with what we commonly call "annuals." They grow, flower, set seed, and die all within a single growing season. Some easy-to-grow annual herbs are basil and dill. Like other annuals, these tend to grow quickly and can provide you with a bountiful harvest. If you faithfully pinch back the developing flowers or deadhead them (remove the faded flowers before they go to seed), many will continue to produce new growth for you to harvest. But when cold, frosty weather begins to threaten, you'd better finish harvesting promptly. Annuals don't wait around. By the end of the season — sometimes earlier — annuals will die.

Some annual herbs, such as cilantro and chervil, are classified as "hardy annuals." Seeds of these annuals can be planted in the fall or very early spring, because they grow despite mild frosts and actually prefer cool weather. They spurt into action in the spring in the North or the winter in the South, and often go to seed in summer.

Biennials. Herbs such as parsley and clary sage are biennials — plants that sprout and produce leafy growth the first year the seed is planted, then flower, produce seed, and subsequently die the second year. Because caraway is a biennial normally grown for its seed, you will have to wait two years to harvest it. On the other hand, parsley is grown for its foliage — and that you will have plenty of in the first year; in the second year it usually bolts quickly, producing little foliage to harvest before it goes to seed.

Perennials. The longest-lived herbs are perennials, plants that last more than two years. How much longer depends on the species and how well it adjusts to the growing conditions. For most success, wait for a year after planting to begin harvesting young perennial herbs. Limit late-summer and fall harvesting in cold climates to avoid encouraging new growth at this time of year — tender new shoots are vulnerable to frost damage, which weakens the whole plant. It is also important to provide growing conditions in which the herb or selected cultivars can thrive. For example, silver-leaved garden sage will grow fairly reliably as far north as zone 5 if given well-drained soil, whereas the golden-variegated cultivar will falter come winter in zone 5.

In colder regions of North America, some plants that are technically perennials are not hardy enough to survive harsh winters. Known as "tender perennials," these plants are sometimes treated as annuals — planted in the garden in spring after danger of frost is past, enjoyed through the summer, and then allowed to die in the fall. If protected from frost and cold temperatures by being brought indoors for the winter, however, these tender perennials will continue to grow for years, as they do in

A Life Cycle Sampler

To help you coordinate your garden, here's a list of some of the herbs that fit different classes of life cycles.

Annual	Biennial	Tender Perennial	Hardy Perennial
Arugula	Angelica	Curry plant	Catnip
Basil	Caraway	French lavender	Lady's mantle
Borage	Chicory	Lemon verbena	Lemon balm
Calendula	Clary sage	Mexican mint marigold	Lovage
Chervil	Parsley	Pineapple sage	Mints
Cilantro	Queen Anne's lace	Rosemary	Salad burnet
Dill		Scented geranium	Sweet cicely
German chamomile		Spanish lavender	Sweet woodruff
Mustard		Sweet bay	Thyme
Nasturtium		Sweet marjoram	Winter savory
Summer savory			Wormwood
			Yarrow

warm southern climates. Examples of tender perennials include some strains of sage and lavender, Mexican mint marigold, scented geraniums, rosemary, and lemon verbena. Many need some rejuvenation in the spring — fresh soil, pruning, or division — to maintain a rigorous pace of growth. Here is a trick for tender perennials: Place the pots in the ground in the spring, burying them up to the rim. Then remove the pot in the fall to bring them indoors.

JUGGLING LIFE CYCLES FOR A BETTER HERB GARDEN

Take advantage of nature's ambiguity to make your herbs last longer or grow better:

- Remove fading flowers to extend the longevity of short-lived herbs. Trick angelica and catnip into growing an additional year by removing their flower stalks and flowers as soon as they emerge. Let a few stems of such annuals as holy basil, dill, and borage go to seed — they'll self-sow and come back year after year.

- Show off perennial and biennial herbs such as sage, rosemary, winter savory, and parsley that retain their foliage into winter. Use their off-season color in knot gardens, edgings, and focal points that you'll cherish when other herbs are dormant. Some herbs offer other kinds of off-season interest — in areas with warm winters such as Dallas, Texas, calendulas will flower all winter.

- Put your annuals in a space separate from your perennials so you can irrigate them in times of drought and rework the soil between plantings without disrupting nearby perennials. But while perennials are young and small, you can temporarily fill the gaps between them with colorful, rapidly growing herbs such as basil and calendula.

- Know which herbs are prolific self-sowers; some examples include mustard, borage, and catnip. Make a point to remove the flowers often to keep these herbs from getting weedy.

- Plant biennials in midsummer, after the first crop of hardy annuals has passed. If your growing season is long enough, they'll be ready to flower the following year — this is fast work for a biennial! When they are done flowering, let your biennials self-sow if you want a perpetual supply.

- Instead of growing tender perennials as annuals, summer them outdoors in pots or in locations where you can easily dig them up and move them into a protected area to escape winter cold.

- To overwinter lemon verbena, try this tip from Steven Foster, an Arkansas-based herbalist. Cut them back severely, then dig the roots up and cover them with moist sand in an unheated cellar for the winter. Potted French lavender needs protection from really cold temperatures,

Summer tender perennials such as bay outdoors.

Both perennial anise hyssop and annual dill generously self-sow.

In Jim Becker's Goodwin Creek Gardens in Oregon, heavy winter rainfall combined with moderate cold causes winter losses. Gardeners in this climate can grow herbs from slightly more southern areas by planting them against a cold frame or lean-to and covering the plants with a clear plastic tent to keep them drier and warmer. Other gardeners use similar self-supporting tents wrapped around bamboo teepees.

but it prefers a cool, bright site such as a cool greenhouse. You will probably want to keep potted rosemary close at hand to use as a fresh herb in winter cooking, but it, too, prefers a cool, bright spot for the winter.

• You can simplify the job of digging up your tender perennials by keeping them in pots when you plant them in the ground. Bury the potted plants up to their rims in garden soil during the summer. This is an especially good idea with herbs such as rosemary that otherwise have very extensive root systems.

• In areas with mild winter frosts such as Texas, tender perennials such as lemon grass and Mexican mint marigolds die back to their roots but generally return again in spring, says herb grower Diane Morey Sitton. Cover plants that don't die back, such as rosemary, with blankets if the temperature is expected to drop more than a few degrees below freezing.

COLD HARDINESS & HEAT TOLERANCE

When the temperature plummets outside, you dress in your winter gear, and you're ready for anything. And when the temperature skyrockets, you can strip down to shorts. But your herbs don't have the same luxuries. They have to make do with whatever your climate throws at them, and their ability to do that is called "hardiness." Hardy plants tolerate heat and cold without wilting or burning in summer or freezing out in winter.

The hardiness zone map is based on the average annual minimum temperatures (how cold it usually gets in your area). So if you live in zone 5, which gets as cold as -10° to -20°F, an herb that is hardy to zone 5 should be good for you. But if a plant is listed only as *half-hardy* in a catalogue, it may not necessarily survive that frigid -20°.

Ask the nursery for more specific temperature recommendations (and perhaps a replacement guarantee) before you buy a plant. You should also check the northern and southern hardiness zone limits for individual plants in Part Five.

© Jerry Howard / Positive Images

An herb garden sheltered in the el of a house is protected against harsh elements.

Winter Cold — The Tip of the Iceberg

Frost strikes the garden in fall, blasting the annuals into blackened skeletons and letting you know that the warm season has come to a close. Then comes extreme cold, the chilliest blasts of winter, turning your perennial herbs into leafless twigs.

No one can argue that cold makes a big impact on your herb garden. But it's mostly a bully with a big bark and a modest bite when it comes to hardy perennial herbs. Several other factors are more likely to threaten your perennial herbs than mere cold weather.

The wind can be a killer — which you already know if you have suffered through frigid wind-chill factors common in northern climates. Blasting wintery wind lowers the effective air temperature, sometimes well below an herb's hardiness level. And it can dry out the exposed foliage on evergreen and semi-evergreen herbs, even during a mild winter. So if you want an herb garden in a wind-swept place, consider blocking the wind with a hedge or vine-covered trellis.

Lavender

"Lavenders don't do well in the southeastern states but not because of high heat alone. It's the humidity that gets them. Lavenders thrive here in Oregon, where temperatures climb over 100 degrees — but it's dry heat," says Jim Becker.

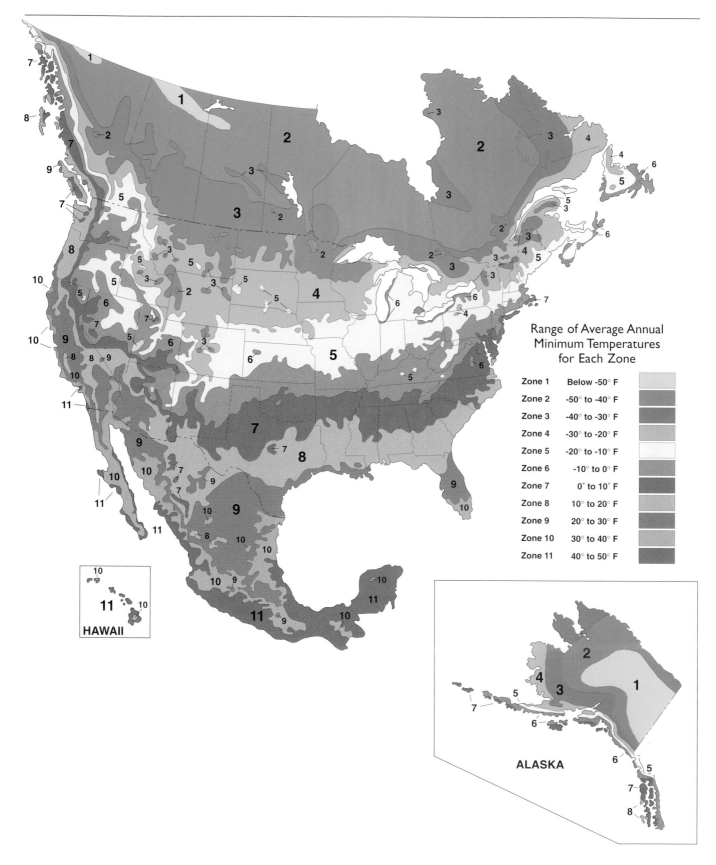

Range of Average Annual
Minimum Temperatures
for Each Zone

Zone 1	Below -50° F
Zone 2	-50° to -40° F
Zone 3	-40° to -30° F
Zone 4	-30° to -20° F
Zone 5	-20° to -10° F
Zone 6	-10° to 0° F
Zone 7	0° to 10° F
Zone 8	10° to 20° F
Zone 9	20° to 30° F
Zone 10	30° to 40° F
Zone 11	40° to 50° F

HAWAII

ALASKA

Winter snows, which might seem a chilly proposition for herbs, actually protect plants. Snow insulates the ground, keeping it safe from rapid temperature drops or extreme cold. If you live in an area with regular snow cover, your hardy herbs will have higher survival rates.

But if you have cool, wet winters, cold and soggy-wet soil, or endless winter rain, herbs can't survive. Being submerged in water or waterlogged soil suffocates herb roots and makes them more susceptible to rotting. This is especially true of the Mediterranean herbs such as thyme, oregano, rosemary, and lavender; they need well-drained soil to last the winter.

Summer Heat and Humidity Also Take a Toll

Unfortunately, hardiness zone maps do not measure summer heat and humidity, which can be just as important as cold when deciding whether a plant will survive more than one season in your area. Many herbs thrive in dry heat — it is just like their Mediterranean homeland. These plants have physically adapted to cope with their native climates. For example, rosemary, winter savory, and lavender have narrow or needlelike leaves that expose less surface area to the sun. Woolly thyme and dittany of Crete are protected by woolly hairs. Lavender and gray santolina have sun-reflecting silver foliage.

Texas Thyme

"I live about 100 miles from the Gulf of Mexico in Texas and have very high humidity," says Diane Morey Sitton. "I love thyme but have to buy new plants every year because the humidity makes them rot out. I also have a lot of trouble with silver-leaved herbs. But lemon grass, which likes a humid, tropical environment, really grows well. *Monarda fistulosa* [wild bergamot], which is beautiful and grows very well, gets mildew many years, although some years are better than others."

© Karen Bussolini / Positive Images

Lavender and gray santolina have sun-reflecting silver foliage, an adaptation that allows them to thrive in dry heat.

Gray-Leaved Herbs

In Steven Foster's zone 6 Arkansas garden, herbs in the Umbelliferae (carrot) Family, such as dill, fennel, parsley, and chervil, grow poorly. "It's just too hot and humid in summer," Foster says. But, he adds, gray-leaved herbs thrive.

But heat can be a problem from zones 6 or 7 to 10, especially when combined with high humidity. Under these conditions, herbs such as sage, sweet woodruff, yarrow, angelica, and chervil tend to fade out quickly. Other herbs such as dill or fennel may grow taller, lankier, and less attractive than they do in the North. Heat can even change the flavor of some herbs, turning garlic, mustard, and cilantro bitter or fiery hot.

In hot and arid climates, broad-leaved, moisture-loving annual herbs can wilt or even die if the soil is too dry. If you live in a hot, arid area, you may want to plant these herbs in light afternoon shade and pay particular attention to watering. (For more details on watering herbs, see page 110.)

Heat combined with high humidity can encourage diseases and become a real problem for many herbs, including bee balm, roses, yarrow, sage, artemisia, gray santolina, and lavender. Such diseases can kill herbs or at least render the harvest unappealing.

MICROCLIMATES

You may find that you can grow a particular herb even if it's not recommended for your area. This is partly because we simply don't know the hardiness limits of every herb, especially the many unusual ones. And since soil and other local conditions can change a plant's survival rate, there is no standard definition of the temperature at which an herb becomes hardy, which accounts for the discrepancies you see in different catalogues. For example, *Salvia clevelandii,* a blue-flowered substitute for garden sage, is listed as hardy in one catalogue but as tender in another.

Hardiness differences also result from variations in weather, site, and climate — some areas are drier and less prone to diseases.

Even those herbs that are fairly thoroughly tested may surprise us when they are grown in ideal conditions. Some gardeners are able to coax a tender plant through winter in a protected location. If you live near a large lake or ocean, winter temperatures can be more moderate. Along the shores of Lake Erie, for example, is zone 6, although just 5 miles inland is zone 5.

Cities also stay warmer than more open country areas. "Large metropolitan areas create a heat dome with all the cement, blacktop, and build-

Stretching Hardiness Limits

To beat the cold

- Don't harvest perennials in fall
- Provide good drainage
- Plant hardy cultivars
- Mulch carefully (see p. 95)
- Plant in a wind-free location
- Warm soil with a black or green plastic mulch before planting
- Plant extra-hardy cultivars
  - 'Arp' and 'Hill Hardy' rosemary
  - 'Green River' parsley
  - 'Hero', 'Hungarian Hot Wax', and 'Super Cayenne' peppers
  - 'Lavender Lady', 'Munstead', and 'Sharon Roberts' lavender

To beat the heat

- Provide good air circulation
- Give light shade in the afternoon
- Avoid high nitrogen fertilizer in summer
- Stick with gentle balanced fertilizers to keep plants healthy and vigorous
- Grow cool-season annuals in winter, fall, or early spring
- Plant heat-resistant herbs
  - 'Ancho', 'Habanero', and 'Anaheim' chile peppers
  - Bronze fennel
  - 'Dukat' dill
  - 'Forest Green' parsley
  - Garlic chives
  - *Lavender grosso* and *Lavender × intermedia*
  - Lemon grass
  - Mexican mint marigold
  - 'Nana' and 'Icterina' garden sage
  - Pineapple sage
- Plant drought-resistant herbs
  - Catnip
  - Germander
  - Gray or green santolina
  - Hyssop
  - Lavender
  - Oregano
  - Rosemary
  - Rue
    Sage
  - Southernwood
  - Sweet Annie artemisia
  - Sweet marjoram
  - Thyme
  - Winter savory
  - Wormwood

ings. Cities can be five to eight degrees warmer than the suburbs in summer and winter both," according to Tony Spicer of the National Weather Service.

He explains that local topography also affects temperature. A garden planted in a low area will be much colder because cold air is dense and drains down to low areas. Such a garden might not last as long as one planted in another area.

A full-sun garden, especially one facing south or west, will be hotter than one in partial sun. A garden in sandy soil in a cold climate will warm up faster in spring and stay better drained in fall and winter, but it will get drier and hotter during summer. A garden in clay soil will stay cooler in spring and more moist in summer, but it will be wetter in winter.

BEFORE YOU PLANT

ind the perfect location for your herb garden, and success is guaranteed. Evaluate the soil, consider the site, and look at sun exposure and shade. Your top priority is finding a site with conditions that will get plants to grow well.

The ideal formula includes equal parts of:

• sun (at least 6 hours a day)

• well-drained soil

• freedom from woody plant roots and erosion

• access to water

• a location that's convenient for you to visit regularly

Begin evaluating garden sites by taking an inventory of the garden conditions. Write them down on paper, just as if you were an accountant. Use cold, hard statistics, such as the number of hours of sun you have and the nature of the soil. Identify liabilities — such as shade, heavy clay, or dry sandy soil. You can turn these liabilities into assets by growing herbs that will thrive there. For example, in a shady yard, you may not be able to grow everything you've dreamed about. But if you realize from the start that the tally sheet for sun exposure has fallen into the red, then you won't waste your money, time, and dreams trying to cultivate a sun-loving herb that just isn't right for the site. Let's break down all the variables in considering your garden site and see what they mean to your herb garden.

SUN EXPOSURE

*A*ll plants need the sun to get down to business, the most important of which is photosynthesizing. Photosynthesis is the process

~

(Opposite page)
Cheerful johnny-jump-ups are among the first blossoms in the spring herb garden.

~

Photo: © Dency Kane

When considering where to start your herb garden, determine where there is full sun between 10 A.M. and 4 P.M.

Shade vs. Sun

"Here in Arkansas, Carrot Family members such as parsley and dill grow best in light shade. Basils can be fine in full sun, as long as you keep them irrigated," says herbalist Steven Foster.

by which plants use solar energy to make food. When this process is roaring along, fueled by plenty of solar radiation, then herbs can begin to produce the good things we grow them for. If light levels are inadequate, herbs may grow skimpy without full flavor, which you'll commonly see in herbs grown indoors in winter.

The exact level of light needed varies with the herb. Most herbs need a full schedule of sun every day to thrive, but others can lounge in the shade and gather enough energy from indirect or filtered sun rays. In very hot or dry conditions, some annual herbs such as dill and parsley grow better if you give them a little relief from the sun.

Let's look at how you can match up your site's sun exposure to the needs of different herbs. Begin by identifying the level of sun exposure.

Sun-loving plants need *full sun,* at least 6 hours of sun falling directly on the garden. So spend a day or two calculating how much sun actually reaches the garden site you're considering. If there are shade trees nearby, do your calculating during the growing season when they are fully leafed out. If sunlight reaches the garden at 10 A.M. and leaves at 4 P.M., you have a winner. But if, during a long midsummer day, the site only gets sun from 8 A.M. to 1 P.M., it will be marginal for sun-loving herbs. With the shorter days in fall and early spring, the sun will be more limited and sun-loving plants will struggle.

If you have a garden that's in *partial sun* — maybe it's beside a building or at the edge of a clump of trees — it will receive 4 to 6 hours of full sun a day. You can use it to grow herbs that tolerate light shade, such as parsley, chives, basil, coriander, and salad burnet. (These plants thrive in full sun but are also successful with less than a full day's worth.) You can also grow plants such as chervil and lady's mantle that thrive in light shade. But if pushed into too dark a location, even shade-tolerant plants can grow tall and lanky, stop flowering, suffer more disease and pest problems, or have diminished flavor.

Sites with less than 4 hours of sun a day can fall into several different categories of shade, which influences which herbs will grow there. *Light shade* locations receive some direct sunlight. Sun may filter through a gap in nearby trees or reach under the tree limbs in the morning and late afternoon. You can use such locations to grow shade-tolerant or shade-

In the Shade

"I grow most things in full sun but find angelica does best in a little shade," says Jim Becker of Oregon's Goodwin Creek Gardens. "I also give tarragon a little bit of shade because I don't think it likes our 100°F summer days too much."

Maximizing Sunlight

If you have your heart set on growing some of the many herbs that thrive in sun-drenched sites — but you have shade — here are some ways to adapt your site.

- Grow herbs in pots that you can set in sunny openings. You can put the containers in a wagon or dolly so you can move them around as the season and sun exposure changes. This may look a little awkward in the middle of the front lawn, but you can do it without embarrassment in the backyard, on a front patio, or along a walk.

- Thin out the tree limbs to let more light filter down to your herb garden. You can have a professional tree trimmer remove lower tree limbs or thin out some branches in the crown. If the trees are not particularly attractive, healthy, or necessary for your landscape design, you might consider removing them altogether.

- To intensify the amount of light that does fall, plant next to a light-colored, sun-reflective structure such as a white building or light gray stone wall that faces south or west.

- Make the most of the spring and fall seasons when your deciduous trees are without leaves. If you have a site shaded by some trees but not overcome with woody roots, use it to grow annuals that love cool weather, such as mustard and cilantro.

- Place your herb garden in the lawn where it won't be shaded by nearby hedges or ornamental shrubs. To blend it in with the rest of the landscape, add a walk or patio beside it or put a fence around it. That way the herb garden becomes an area for walking and sitting, as well as enjoying your herbs in the kitchen.

When Shade Is a Benefit

Although shade limits the number of plants you can grow, light shade has some advantages, too. It will keep herbs — especially those that prefer cool, moist conditions — from overheating, wilting, and losing quality in summer's heat. It may allow you to grow plants that usually grow further to the north, in cooler climates, especially if you keep the soil moist and mulched.

loving plants such as mints, sweet woodruff, violets, and sweet cicely.

Heavy shade, found under evergreen trees or thickly branched deciduous trees, receives little or no direct sunlight. You will be severely limited in your choice of herbs that will grow here.

There are other factors to consider besides hours of sunlight when evaluating shade. A shadow cast by a tree can be different than a shadow cast by a structure. The shade that falls beside a wall or building lasts all year, whereas shade surrounding deciduous trees vanishes when the leaves fall. The shade beside structures may be accompanied by moist, damp soil and stagnant air, which encourage disease, slugs, or snails. But the shade near many trees — especially silver maples and beeches — can be riddled with aggressive tree roots, which parch the soil and make it doubly difficult to grow herbs.

© Dency Kane

A sunny garden site gets at least 6 hours of direct sunlight.

SLOPE

*D*oes your yard have a gentle or steep slope, or is it perfectly flat? Determine which characterizes your yard because it could influence how your herb garden grows.

Flat Land. A flat garden can be a very effective one. When moistened by rain or irrigation, the soil absorbs water where it has fallen, giving every plant its fair share. But a very flat site can be visually monotonous. It helps to break it up with taller plants, trellises, fences or hedges, and raised beds.

Gentle Incline. A slight slope can provide a beautiful showcase for herbs. Those uphill will stand out more prominently. But a slope also allows some differences in soil moistness. Water will tend to seep down to the lower levels, leaving the uphill portions of the slope well drained and slightly drier.

© judywhite

Shallow terraces are an effective treatment for a gentle slope.

Steep Slope. Hilly land can be hard to cultivate. It can also be hard to work in, especially if you have to haul around wheelbarrow loads of supplies. Water will run off rapidly, carrying away valuable topsoil and even hard underlayers of the soil. To stop erosion and give cultivated herbs a chance to get a foothold, install some terraces that elevate portions of the slope to make the planting beds less steep.

Hillside. If you have the pleasure of choosing a garden site anywhere along the gentle slope of a hill, you'll find conditions are quite different from the top to the bottom.

Hilltops. Hilltops tend to be colder because they are windswept — and this can spell trouble for herbs that remain exposed in winter. Wind can cause them to dry out and die back or die altogether. So, plan to protect them by blocking the wind with a burlap wrap or a windscreen such as a hedge, vine-covered fence, or trellis.

Gardens situated in valleys at the base of hills tend to have more problems with early or late frosts. Frost tends to roll down inclines and collect in low areas. This may damage the herbs that emerge early in spring or cut short your harvest season in fall. You can limit frost damage, however, by covering your plants temporarily with sheets, plastic, burlap, or plant quilts whenever frost threatens.

The middle portion of a slope is a more gentle location for a garden. The site may stay warmer than hilltop and lower sites by avoiding the wind at the top and the frost pockets at the bottom.

SOIL COMPOSITION

One of the most wonderful things about wiggling your toes in the warm sand on a beach is feeling it shift and trickle over your skin. You can thank the coarse texture of the sand for that pleasure. It keeps sand loose and flowing.

If, in contrast, you step barefoot into a pile of moist clay, you may never forget feeling it ooze coolly between your toes and coat your feet. Clay's slippery, slimy texture when wet comes from its ultra-fine particles. The same particles, when dry, can pack hard together and make brick.

The textures that create different feelings underfoot will also make a big difference in how your plants grow. Looser soils (those that contain at least 35 percent sand) allow water to run through faster. They stay drier and better aerated but are lower in nutrients. They can also be quicker to warm up in spring.

Soils that are at least 30 percent clay act differently. They tend to hold moisture and nutrients, and so they are likely to be more fertile. But those tiny particles can be so tightly packed that there's little elbow room for air. When submerged in soggy soil, herbs are more prone to problems with diseases.

Now let's consider the middleground, a loam soil. Loam is a blend of sand, clay, and medium-sized particles called "silt." Their characteristics vary depending on the proportion of sand or clay.

In a productive garden, you'll also have organic matter softening and enriching the mineral elements, rather like egg in a sponge cake. Organic matter, such as skeletonized leaves, softening twigs, and fibrous remains of decaying wood, is coarse enough to help keep even tight clay soil loose and light. It also holds moisture and releases a trickle of nutrients that can fortify sandy soils. Unlike mineral elements, organic matter decays quickly. You'll have to add more every year. Work compost, peat moss, or old rotting straw and seedless weeds and grass clippings into the soil in the fall or use it as mulch.

Soil Testing

To find out what your garden soil is like, get a feel for what levels of sand and clay your garden contains. When you grasp a handful of soil, if it feels soft and slippery it's sure to contain some clay. If it feels gritty it includes some sand.

For a more precise picture, squeeze a handful of moist soil into a ball, then work a ribbon of the soil out between your thumb and forefinger. If the ribbon gets to be an inch or longer, you have clay soil. If it's just under an inch long, you have clay loam (a mix of clay and silt). If it breaks off at ½ to ¼ inch, it's an intermediate loamy blend. If it breaks up before forming much of a ribbon, your soil is sandy.

For a more specific soil structure test, put a cup of soil in a quart jar and fill it to the top with distilled water. Screw the top on tightly. Shake the jar until the water is cloudy and no residue clings to the bottom of the jar. Then put the jar on a counter and set a timer for 5 minutes. When the alarm goes off, measure the thickness of the soil layer that has settled in the bottom of the jar. That's the amount of sand in the soil. Reset the alarm for 55 minutes so you can measure the next layer, which is silt. The last layer, clay, will take the rest of the day to settle.

You also can get a feel for your soil type by checking soil drainage, the potential for water to move through the soil. Usually water drains faster from sandy soils if the moisture isn't blocked by unseen hard layers beneath the soil. Dig a hole about a foot deep in your garden and fill it with water. Let the water drain out, refill the hole, and wait for eight hours. If the hole isn't empty, you may need to add some extra sand or organic matter to make the soil lighter. You also may need to raise the bed if it's in a low area, break up compacted subsurface soil layers, or add a drainage ditch or underground drainage tiles.

Caraway

Soil Fertility

Many of the classic herbs need very little, if any, fertilizer. It's true that plants need nutrients to grow. But nutrients only grease the wheels of growth — they don't power it. If applied in excess, they can burn plant roots, mimic diseases, and ruin the quality of your herb harvest.

Provide enough nutrients to prevent shortages, but don't fall into the trap of giving herbs too many nutrients. In many cases you can get good plant growth simply by upgrading your soil. Get to know the different nutrients so you can use them wisely.

Macronutrients. Plants use a variety of nutrients, including macronutrients such as nitrogen, potassium, and phosphorus. These three elements, and about a dozen others needed in smaller quantities, are usually available in soils that are rich in organic matter such as compost, leaf humus, or decayed livestock manure. If you find your soil is deficient, you'll need to add whatever is limited to get good herb growth.

- Nitrogen (N) helps plants grow lush and produce dark green leaves. Without it, foliage will yellow and growth will slow or stop. Some fertilizers provide nitrogen in water-soluble forms that plants absorb and respond to quickly but that may wash out of the soil following frequent or heavy rains. Organic fertilizers may release some of their nitrogen more gradually as the organic source slowly decomposes in the soil.

- Phosphorus (P) promotes general good health as well as root, flower, and seed production. If limited, plants will have stunted growth and dark, purple-tinted leaves. Phosphorus is generally held in an insoluble form in the soil and released slowly through natural degradation by soil organisms. Because it doesn't wash through the soil like nitrogen, you should work amendments containing phosphorus throughout the bed before planting so that the deeper burrowing roots will also have access.

- Potassium (K) is vital for vigorous, healthy plants that resist diseases and produce abundant seeds. Without it, plants may be stunted and sickly. The older leaves may turn bronze-colored and the stems may become floppy.

Nutrient Testing

In many states, you can get an inexpensive soil test done by the Cooperative Extension Service, often listed under county or federal government offices in the yellow pages. For more detailed nutrient analysis, you can send soil samples to a private laboratory recommended by your Extension agent.

© Rosalind Creasy

In a raised bed, you can upgrade soil with organic matter (e.g., compost, leaf humus, peat moss, or manure). Here tarragon, nepeta, and sage thrive in raised beds.

Micronutrients, needed in such tiny amounts that they may actually be toxic to plants if present in abundance, are available in most organic rich soils and some organic fertilizers. They include copper (Cu), manganese (Mn), iron (Fe), calcium (Ca), and zinc (Zn), which are part of plant enzymes; sulfur (S), which is part of plant proteins; magnesium (Mg), which is important for photosynthesis; and molybdenum (Mo) and boron (B), which help other nutrients work.

The Importance of pH

Have you ever eaten garden-fresh tomatoes meal after meal and day after day? Eventually, your stomach may develop a sensitivity to the tomato acidity, which measures around 4.5 on the pH scale of 1 to 14. The pH of your garden soil is a useful measurement for revealing which nutrients are available in your garden.

On the pH scale, 1 to 6.9 indicate acidic soil; 7 indicates neutral soil; and 7.1 to 14 indicates alkaline soil. Levels lower than 4 or higher than 9 would be next to impossible to garden in because essential nutrients are locked into the soil. Fortunately, such conditions are extremely rare.

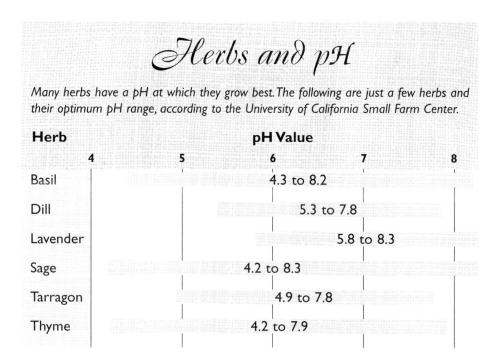

Herbs and pH

Many herbs have a pH at which they grow best. The following are just a few herbs and their optimum pH range, according to the University of California Small Farm Center.

Herb	pH Value
	4 5 6 7 8
Basil	4.3 to 8.2
Dill	5.3 to 7.8
Lavender	5.8 to 8.3
Sage	4.2 to 8.3
Tarragon	4.9 to 7.8
Thyme	4.2 to 7.9

Most herbs will grow best in moderate pH levels, between 6 and 7.5. A pH of 6.5 is something of a magic number because it represents the pH at which the greatest number of nutrients are available. This pH is excellent for chives, basil, onions, horseradish, mustard, parsley, peppers, sage, thyme, and most other herbs. Lavender, which is reputed to love more alkaline conditions, also thrives at a pH of 6.5 or even slightly lower.

Amending your soil pH is a long-term commitment. You can add products to change the pH, but they are all short-term solutions. You'll have to recheck the pH every year or two and adjust it as necessary. To make an alkaline soil more acidic, you can add sulfur, pine needles, or peat moss. To make an overly acidic soil more alkaline, add lime. Try sprinkling very acidic soil with lime until the white powder lightly covers the surface. Follow package directions to get the best results.

Improving Soil

If your soil is a productive loam, your easiest option is to leave well enough alone and grow herbs that will thrive in your soil type. But if your soil is not what you want it to be, try the following suggestions.

To Change Soil Texture. Work amendments through a wide area so plants can grow and spread freely. A little sand added to heavy clay soil won't improve drainage. Rainwater will drain quite nicely through the sand, only to collect within the walls of the clay hole. If you only add a bucket of organic matter to an individual plant site, roots may have difficulty growing from the amended area into the surrounding soil. So when you amend, do it right with the following formulas.

- To lighten heavy clay soil, work 25 percent coarse sand into the entire bed, a 3-inch layer for a 12-inch-deep bed. Also add a layer of compost, at least an inch or two thick. Add an inch or more annually.

- To enrich a sandy soil, work in a layer of organic matter 3 to 6 inches deep when you first cultivate the bed. Continue to add an inch or two every year afterward.

To Improve Drainage. In a site that's overly wet for at least a portion of the year, look into the specific cause of the problem. If the site is in a low spot, you can raise the garden by adding extra topsoil so water won't accumulate there. You can take this idea a step further by containing the bed in rocks, logs, bricks, or cement blocks so you can raise the planting area 10 inches to several feet high. The higher you make the bed, the drier the upper levels of soil will become.

Sometimes water overflows from your gutters and makes the garden area too wet. This is easy to solve by cleaning the old leaves and birds' nests out of your gutter regularly so water can flow through it, instead of flooding over it. It's also smart to plant herbs that need good drainage well away from the gutter drip line, just in case you get a little behind.

Water seeping out of a water line or underground spring can also saturate the soil. To correct these problems, you may need to fix your underground plumbing or install drainage pipes below the surface of the soil. Drainage pipes capture extra water and send it down to your storm sewer or to a culvert or stream.

Adding Organic Matter. Soil is alive with worms, moles, grubs, and larvae that we can see and bacteria, fungi, and microbes we can't see. These beneficial creatures aerate the soil, consume decaying matter, release nutrients, and coat and protect plant roots. Some fungi extend plant roots — drawing in depleted nutrients. But other microorganisms prey upon plants, causing declines and diseases when conditions are right for their attack.

Your goal is to develop soil that encourages beneficial organisms and discourages disease organisms. To do this, you need to maintain at least 5 percent organic matter in the soil at any given time. This quantity of organic matter holds moisture and releases nutrients, nourishes microscopic soil allies, and reaps your herbs many rewards. Organic matter is constantly being broken down into nutrient soup, a process that moves especially quickly in warm climates and sandy soil. To replace what's decomposed, create your own compost and add at least 1 inch of it (or leaf humus or well-decayed, aged livestock manure) to a garden every year. Work it into the soil in new beds or use it as a topdressing on existing beds.

Compost, Super Soil Booster

Among the best things you can do for your soil is to add compost — soft, crumbly, brown, predigested yard and stable waste. Compost nourishes a healthy soil, which passes its strength along to plants. It contains a smorgasbord of macro- and micronutrients that are released slowly in quantities plants can use gradually. Compost holds moisture, feeds beneficial organisms in soil, lightens and loosens heavy soils, and enriches light soils. What's even better is that you can make it for free.

Organize a carefully prepared pile for quick compost or a random, toss-as-you-go pile to harvest a couple years from now.

Fast, Hot Compost. This is the way to go if you want to get the best compost possible in the shortest amount of time — and you don't mind doing some extra work to make it all come about. Collect several kinds of yard waste to make an ideal organic blend. Find hard or brown matter: fallen leaves, straw, ground-up wood chips. Add soft or green matter: grass clippings, lettuce leaves, livestock manure. These provide nitrogen to feed microscopic decomposers. Avoid weedy seeds or yard scraps that are diseased or full of insects. These problems might survive composting and return to plague your garden.

Sandwich your compost, alternating 4 inches of dry, brown material between 2-inch layers of soft, green material. If it is high-carbon material

This simple wooden composting bin allows oxygen to reach all sides of the pile of organic matter. Some gardeners have two compost bins — while the first pile decays, a second pile can be started.

The open brickwork on this three-sided compost bin allows oxygen to reach all sides of the pile. The open fourth side makes access easy for turning the compost with a pitchfork as it decays. Turning the compost with a pitchfork is beneficial because it blends and aerates, which speeds up decomposition.

such as wood chips or sawdust, increase the width of the soft, green layer or add extra nitrogen fertilizer. After experimenting with different layers a time or two, you'll begin to get a feel for the quantities that get decay moving fast and hot.

Build the mound up until it reaches 3 feet high and wide. Contain the pile in wire mesh or snow fencing, or leave it in a heap. To increase the amount of oxygen that penetrates the pile, you will need to encourage decomposers and mix the ingredients, turning the pile with a pitchfork every couple weeks. Or, for the ultimate in convenience, put the compost into a compost-making machine that cranks, rotates, or rolls around to blend and aerate the pile.

Your compost is finished when it's brown and crumbly and you can't identify the original components.

Slow, Comfortable Compost. Cold composting doesn't heat up as it decays. It may take a couple of years to break down, but it eventually serves its purpose.

With cold compost, be especially careful to omit disease, insect- or seed-infested yard scraps. If you have the time and inclination, you could separate your soft green and hard brown matter and layer them as indicated

Other Sources of Compost

If you can't make as much compost as you need, you can get extra. Here are some ways to look for compost.

- Call City Hall. Some communities have their own composting programs and a few of them give away the compost free or at a low cost to local residents.
- Call the Cooperative Extension Service, often listed under federal or county offices in the phone book. Your agricultural agent probably knows who is composting in your area.
- Call a nearby landscaper or nursery. Companies that collect leaves in the fall may stockpile them and let them decay. If they have more than they need, they may sell or give some to you.
- Call a nearby stable. They may have some old manure piled up somewhere that they'd love to give away. Or, if they don't, they may have been hauling the manure to a composting facility that they can recommend to you.
- Call a bulk soil dealer. Many of the larger soil dealers are also selling compost or a premium-priced blend of compost and topsoil.
- As a last resort, for a smaller garden you can buy bags of leaf humus or composted cow manure. These are often on sale at large lawn and garden dealers, so you can get a dozen or more bags affordably.

in fast, hot composting. But even if you don't, sooner or later everything will decay. If you're adding a lot of hard, brown material, sprinkle it with a little nitrogen fertilizer — some blood meal or fish emulsion. Continue to add to the pile until it reaches 3 feet high or an entire growing season passes. Then leave that pile to decay and start a new one. (If you keep heaping more scraps on the top, you'll have a hard time getting at the decayed compost at the bottom.)

CHAPTER 5

DESIGNING YOUR HERB GARDEN

W ell-grown herbs look even more stunning when used in a handsome design complemented by walks, walls, or accessories. A design also makes your garden much more than simply a place to grow plants. It becomes a fragrant, colorful, and comfortable outdoor place to sit, read, play, and entertain, and it grows into an asset that increases your property value.

The design style you choose says a lot about your preferences and personality. Try a historical garden if you like a sense of tradition. Or install a classic formal herb garden, a look that never goes out of date. If you prefer to grow a wide variety of plants in a casual way, develop an informal cottage garden. Or tailor a contemporary garden to fit into small spaces or blend in with the rest of your landscape.

Read on in this chapter for ideas on how to pull together a beautiful and effective herb garden design. You'll learn how to make herb combinations that look and grow well together. Then you'll deal with woody plants, the supporting characters that give herb gardens height, structure, and character during winter. You'll be ready to devote some thought to your hardscape — all the walks, walls, and other built structures in your garden. Then browse through some possible designs, and consider taking what you've learned and adding some low-maintenance features.

DESIGN CONSIDERATIONS

W hen you know which herbs you want to plant, think about how you can arrange them so they'll look great and grow their best. Consider their color and ornamental characteristics, time of bloom,

~

(Opposite page)

The colorfully contrasting foliage of santolina, rosemary, artemisia, germander, rue, and boxwood is used to create a traditional herb garden design.

~

Photo: © Lee Anne White / Positive Images

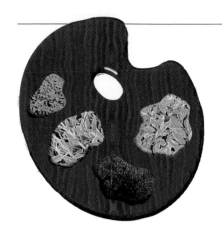

height, and growth habits. Then imagine how the characteristics of each herb will look when combined with another herb. You can plant contrasting herbs in nearby parts of the garden to show off bold and subtle colors, large and small leaves, tall spikes of flowers and low carpets of blossoms. Plan to have enough diversity to make the garden interesting but also enough repetition of similar characteristics to tie the garden together and keep it harmonious — not chaotic.

Coordinating Color in Your Herb Garden

Herbs come in a wide range of flower and foliage colors, all of which are important to your garden design. Often, the most effective plant combinations come from simple color schemes — two or three main colors repeated throughout the garden. The colors you choose can be similar or contrasting, depending on how soothing or vibrant you want the garden to be.

To include a wider range of color, you can divide the garden into sections, as with the Four-Square or Wagon Wheel designs (see p. 63). You can use a different color scheme in each section.

A Glossary of Design Terms

As you start planning and designing your herb garden, there are some concepts it will help you to become familiar with. Color and texture are key concepts, but consider also the finer distinctions.

Colors. Colors make a big impact on the garden, so organize your color scheme carefully.

Hue. This is the tint or underlying tones in a color — such as orange-red or yellow-orange. Sometimes, colors that are tinted with hues of yellow, such as salmon pink, don't look great with colors tinted with hues of blue, such as lavender-pink.

Complementary Colors. Bold color combinations can combine warm and cool colors using opposites on the color wheel such as red with green, blue with orange, and yellow with purple.

Analogous Color. More subtle color combinations use neighboring colors on the color wheel such as orange, yellow, and red, or purple, blue, and green.

Texture. This is the distinctive character created by the size, shape, and finish of plant leaves.

Coarse. Large, full leaves as on lettuce-leaf basil, and large, stiffly branched plants such as angelica and lovage are coarse-textured and bold eye attractors.

Fine. Narrow, small, or finely cut, smooth leaves such as winter savory, thyme, and dill give a soft look but can become busy if used in quantities.

Medium. Moderate-sized leaves such as mint and sweet basil are comfortable to view but monotonous in large quantities.

© William Adams

© William Adams

(Left) The unusual violet hues of bronze fennel makes it a useful complement to a variety of other herbs.

(Right) These variegated sages are a colorful contrast to the silvery santolina.

Tried-and-true color combinations, like the ones that follow, look great in any garden. But don't be afraid to experiment. Hold nursery plants close together to see if the combination is visually pleasing, or move your existing garden plants around to create new, more interesting color combinations. Remember, everyone has different color preferences, so there is no right or wrong

Combine colorful foliage with colorful flowers. The silver foliage of artemisias, santolina, sage, lavender, and other herbs looks good with the cool-colored blue or purple flowers of chives and sage and also with pastel pink flowers.

Bronze- and gold-leaved herbs such as bronze fennel, golden oregano, and golden variegated sage look great with warm-colored yellow, orange, and red flowers such as 'Lemon Gem' and 'Orange Gem' marigolds, nasturtiums, and pineapple sage.

But not everyone is fond of purple- or bronze-leaved herbs. Some gardeners prefer to use purple foliage with discretion. One objection to purple- and dark-leaved herbs is that they become less noticeable when the light fades at dusk or in a shaded site.

Match the color of flowers to highlight color on a variegated leaf. Try 'Pink Ripple' thyme with matching 'Tricolor' sage leaves, or a yellow-flowered

© David Cavagnaro

© Rosalindi Creasy

(Left) Richly toned 'Purple Ruffles' basil is a dramatic foil for bright red and white annuals and 'Silver White' salvia.

(Right) Scented geranium, thyme, lamb's ears, and lavender grow in terraces alongside a set of steps.

nasturtium with golden variegated sage or golden lemon balm. Or use white-flowered garlic chives or white-flowered rosemary with 'Argenteus' silver thyme, white-variegated calamint, or 'Snowflake' scented geranium. Match the blue-green leaves of rue with the blue flowers of borage, blue sage *(Salvia Clevelandii),* or hyssop. A more subtle combination is purple-flowered 'Marshall's Delight' bee balm with purple-stemmed 'Chocolate' peppermint.

Jim Wilson recommends that to get the best display with the most colorful herbs, such as 'Tricolor' sage, grow them next to a plain-looking herb. One good combination is 'Tricolor' sage with 'Spicy Globe' basil, which forms a neat green mound and grows to about the same height.

Mix herbs with dark- and light-colored foliage if you like a lot of contrast. For example, place a mass of five or seven plants of silvery sage as a backdrop behind five dark purple basil and a couple of yellow nasturtium. Or use 'Silver King' artemisia in the back of the bed, purple perilla in front of it, and 'Silver Mound' artemisia as an edging plant in the foreground. Holly Shimizu highlights purple foliage with silver, blending tall pink-flowered mountain mint with purple-leaved perilla, dwarf gray santolina, and cascading lemon thyme.

If this is too much contrast for your liking, try silver foliage with dark green foliage. Gray or silver herbs such as 'Powis Castle' artemisia beside

Flowering Sequence

Plants	Spring	Summer	Fall
Calendula	▨▨▨▨▨		
Chives	▨▨▨▨▨		
Dianthus	▨▨▨▨▨		
Lamb's ears	▨▨▨▨▨		
Mustard	▨▨▨▨▨		
Sweet woodruff	▨▨▨▨▨		
Violas	▨▨▨▨▨		
Anise hyssop		▨▨▨▨	
Artemisia		▨▨▨▨	
Basil		▨▨▨▨▨▨	
Bee balm		▨▨▨▨	
Borage		▨▨▨▨	
Catmint		▨▨▨▨	
Chamomile		▨▨▨▨	
Coriander		▨▨▨▨	
Dill		▨▨▨▨	
Fennel		▨▨▨▨▨▨	
Feverfew		▨▨▨▨	
Lavender		▨▨▨▨▨▨	
Lemon balm		▨▨▨▨	
Lovage		▨▨▨▨	
Marigold		▨▨▨▨	
Mint		▨▨▨▨	
Nasturtium		▨▨▨▨▨▨	
Old-fashioned rose		▨▨▨▨	
Oregano		▨▨▨▨	
Rue		▨▨▨▨	
Sage		▨▨▨▨	
Scented geranium		▨▨▨▨▨▨	
Sweet marjoram		▨▨▨▨	
Thyme		▨▨▨▨	
Valerian		▨▨▨▨	
Yarrow		▨▨▨▨	
Calendula			▨▨▨▨
Garlic chives			▨▨▨▨
Pineapple sage			▨▨▨▨
Saffron			▨▨▨▨

any dark green plant are a lovely combination. For even less contrast, combine the many shades of green.

Color through the Seasons

An herb garden composed of a variety of interesting kinds of herb foliage will always look good. But you can make the garden look even better if you organize herb companions that will flower in sequence — spring, summer, and fall (see chart, p. 47). In addition to providing color and cut flowers, most herb blossoms attract beneficial insects that help to keep your entire landscape pest-free. (If you harvest some herbs before they flower, you'll have to leave them out of the flowering sequence.)

Texture

Flowers come and go, but leaves make their mark on the herb garden throughout the growing season — and sometimes beyond. In addition to the varying shades of green, gray, gold, and purple of some herbs, you can make your garden more satisfying by including herbs with intriguing vari-

© William Adams

Plant herbs together that have variations in texture. The contrasting textures of coconut and woolly thymes make an interesting ground cover.

ations in texture. Texture is the distinctive character created by the size, shape, and finish of plant leaves.

Fine-textured plants are those with narrow, small, or finely cut smooth leaves such as winter savory or thyme. They have a dainty look that softens the garden, but they can become too busy if used in large numbers. Medium-textured plants are those with moderate-sized leaves such as mint and sweet basil. They fill space comfortably, but they can become boring if overused. Coarse-textured plants have large and full leaves as on lettuce-leaf basil and large, stiffly branched plants such as angelica and lovage. These make bold eye attractors.

Blend these textures to fit the ambiance of your garden. You can't go wrong if you emphasize medium-textured plants, but highlight them occasionally with clumps of fine-textured plants or small, bold groups of coarse-textured plants. Or, in small spaces, emphasize fine-textured plants with some bolder herbs for accent. In a large garden far from the house, take advantage of a large percentage of large and coarse-textured herbs, which will make the garden appear closer.

Making Masses

If you like the look of one particular herb, magnify it by planting that herb in clusters or large masses that give it extra power through size. Massing is particularly important if you intermingle herbs into landscape beds where they can be lost among large trees and shrubs. Large masses let your eye flow over the entire garden; they don't become busy and chaotic. Set one species or cultivar in groups of three, five, seven, or nine, depending on the size of the bed and how much use you have for that plant. Let the mass drift across the background or foreground of the garden.

Varying Heights

In my garden, arugula leaves routinely grow to about 6 inches high. But in my friend's garden, they stretch up a lush 10 inches because the soil is so rich. In my Cleveland, Ohio, garden, sweet basil gets to be about 2 feet high. But on Jim Wilson's South Carolina farm, it can get taller. Variations in height are not a rare occurrence. Herbs can and will break the rules.

Here low-growing 'Piccolo Verde' basil is massed in front of *Salvia farinacea* and purple basil.

© judywhite

There are several reasons for this. Rich soil, warm weather, and/or some shade will make some herbs grow taller. Leaner and drier soil in full sun will keep most herbs more compact. So will pinching, shearing, and growing herbs in snug containers. You'll also see variation in height among different cultivars of the same herb, herbs that are grown from seed, and uncommon herbs that have a lot of natural variation.

You'll also find that height is a flexible thing. You can prune some medium-sized herbs shorter and use them as foreground plants. Or, you can cut back some taller plants and maintain them at a medium height. You may

Getting the Visual Effect

Organize herbs roughly by height so the garden will build from low to high and nothing will be hidden. If you'll be looking at your herbs from only one direction — for instance, if the garden is in front of a hedge or wall — then you'll want the shorter plants in the front and the taller plants in the back. In a garden that you view from all sides, place the taller plants in the center and the lower plants around the perimeter.

Try not to be too rigid when you make tiers of shorter and taller plants. In informal gardens, you can intermingle heights slightly and still maintain the rhythm of gradually increasing heights. Let a ribbon of medium-sized plants snake into areas with low and tall plants. Or frame some beautiful lower-growing herb plants between taller plants so you peer through the opening to see them. You also can put short or medium high, early-spring-blooming plants in the back of the garden, where they'll put on a show while the taller plants are still dormant or just beginning to grow.

also notice, if you have warm weather or rich soil, that some normally low-growing herbs may shoot up taller and may reach into the medium height range. Here are some herbs of different heights, with suggestions on how to incorporate them in your design.

Creeping Herbs. Herbs up to several inches high such as Corsican mint and creeping thyme that shimmy close to the ground can weave amid the stones or bricks in a walk. Pave with irregularly shaped pieces of flagstone instead of rectangular pieces to encourage openings between the stones in which you can plant the creeping herbs.

Low, Edging Herbs. Lower-growing plants up to about 12 inches tall can line the edge of the garden or rest at the feet of a taller plant. Use small plants with tidy growth habits — such as 'Spicy Globe' basil, curly parsley, 'Silver Mound' artemisia, Roman chamomile, thyme, lady's mantle, winter savory, betony (without the flowers), gray or green santolina (if clipped), alpine strawberries, dwarf sage, and woolly yarrow — to form lines and curves at the edge of the garden. Stick with one or two kinds of herbs in the edging to give the garden a distinct form and a sense of unity.

Get to know a prospective edging plant well before you make a commitment to use a lot of it. The perfect edging is one you use in abundance, perhaps parsley or alpine strawberries, because you'll have plenty to harvest. It should also be an herb that stays neat through the growing season — or better yet, beyond. Some herbs look good at the start of spring but

Neat Edgings Make Tidy Gardens

Tend edging plants carefully. Keep them well manicured even if the rest of the garden is a little less well groomed. The edge is often the first thing a visitor sees, and it leaves the greatest impression.

get scraggly later. Others take a long time to regenerate after a cold winter, and their barren stems detract from the beauty of the spring garden. Try to find an edger that avoids these flaws in your climate. You can also look for edging herbs with colors and textures that complement nearby companion herbs. Finally, for a really knock-out edging along paths, choose fragrant herbs that will cascade out onto the walkway and fill the air with perfume when you brush by.

Medium Height Herbs. Herbs 13 to 24 inches high include most basils, calendula, caraway, German chamomile, chervil, chives, coriander, hyssop, lavender, lemon balm, Mexican mint marigold, sweet marjoram, most mints, Greek oregano, compact rosemary cultivars, summer savory, and sage. These plants can fill in the middle spaces of a broad garden or the rear of a narrow garden. They have enough substance to work well in many other parts of the landscape, as well as in the herb garden.

Tall Herbs. For this definition, tall herbs include plants over 2 feet high to as tall as 6 feet high. They can be narrowly upright, bushy and vase shaped, or just plain big and bold. This category includes plants such as wormwood, southernwood, bronze fennel, upright-growing scented geraniums such as 'Citronella' and 'Lemon Balm', perilla, Russian sage *(Perovskia atriplicifolia),* roses, most rosemary cultivars, rue, pineapple sage, French tarragon, and valerian. But these herbs may not retain their full height all season long. Lovage, French sorrel, Florence fennel, and angelica, for instance, reach their full height when they flower. Other herbs such as bee balm, yarrow, and borage have the potential to be tall if they don't flop. You may have to support them with stakes, wire rings, or grow-through wire grids to take advantage of their height.

If you work with herbs in the taller range, remember that a tall herb in a narrow bed looks awkward and out of place unless planted near a tall pole, wall, statue, or similar feature. To make the plants look natural, limit the height of the tallest herb to half the diameter of the garden. Keep tall herbs trimmed back to a lower size, if necessary.

CHARTING HERBS —
A PLANNING TOOL

If you neglect to organize your herbs before planting, you're sure to have some mix-ups. Tall plants will erupt up front and short plants will be lost behind them. These kinds of mistakes are easy to avoid if you chart plant characteristics before you plant. Use these charts to double check your garden plan and make sure it is going to work as well as you had hoped.

Begin by looking up each herb's vital statistics in the Grower's Guide that begins on page 177. Then on a piece of paper (accounting paper is good), set up different columns under headings such as Plant Name (or Cultivar), Height (this could be a range), Season of Bloom (spring, summer, or fall), Color (foliage or flower, including hue if needed), and Other Ornamental Features (texture, fragrance, or form). List plants you intend to group near each other in the chart and fill in as much information as you can. Then scan down each column and see if an herb will be tall or short enough, and if the colors and other features will work together. Here's an example for a small garden:

Name	Height	Season	Color	Other
Parsley	12"	all	green	frilly leaves
'Whirlybird' Nasturtium	12"	summer	yellow or red	round leaves
Golden Variegated Sage	18"	all	gold/green	leathery leaves
Achillea x 'Coronation Gold'	36"	summer	gold	large showy flowers
Lovage	48"– 60"	mid-summer	yellow	bold texture

Complementary Herbs

You can intermingle herbs within the same growing space, just as you can plant ivy under deciduous shrubs or trees. This lets you make maximum use of your garden space and intensify your design with varying layers of plants, colors, and textures.

For example, underplant shrub roses with fragrant mints or lemon balm, which help deter rose pests. Or let tall, purple-flowered stars-of-Persia *(Allium christophii)* emerge through a low, pink- or purple-flowered thyme such as 'Pink Ripple' or 'Linear Leaf Lilac'. In light shade, underplant tall angelica with lady's mantle for an interesting contrast in leaf texture and flowers during spring and summer.

If you select companion herbs carefully, they can benefit each other's growth. For instance, the tallest herb should be sun-loving; the lower herb should tolerate some shade. Then they can both get a fair share of sunlight. Better yet, if one is deep rooted and the other is shallow rooted, they can divide up rooting space with little competition.

If you don't put enough thought into finding suitable companions for close plantings or if you start with marginal growing conditions, the plants may end up competing for sun, moisture, and nutrients. Both plants could

© Rosalind Creasy

Tall-growing oregano provides some shade for annual lobelia.

suffer and so could your harvest. If you have doubts about compatibility, experiment on a small scale at first.

WOODY PLANTS TO ENHANCE HERB GARDENS

*U*se herbal or purely ornamental shrubs or small trees to frame your garden and provide height. Woody limbs have graceful shapes and evergreen leaves have lasting colors that endure through both summer and winter. The branches of trees and shrubs stretch over or around other plants, elevating and enclosing the garden. Trees with fine leaves and open branching cast light shade that protects nearby plants that can't take full sun or intense heat.

In the right places, woody plants can be useful in nearly any herb garden. Compact or easily sheared shrubs such as boxwood or small-leaved Japanese hollies can make a clipped hedge around a formal garden. Taller evergreen shrubs such as hollies, yews, and junipers are good as hedges to frame at least part of the garden. For height in corners (and for flowers to

© Ivan Masser / Positive Images

Non-herbs, such as ornamental grasses and bright poppies, combine well with herbs in this lively garden.

dry for potpourri), add roses, lilacs, forsythias, hydrangeas, fothergillas, or viburnums. Where height and a little shade would be welcome over a bench in the garden, try fragrant tree lilacs, linden trees with flowers that make wonderful tea, or witch hazel, a medicinal herb.

What kinds of woody plants should you use? In warm climates, try shrubby herbs such as rosemary and sweet bay. Or substitute ornamentals such as camellia, aucuba, beautyberry, glory-bower, gardenia, heavenly bamboo, pittosporum, or crape myrtle. In cooler climates, substitute hardy shrubs such as boxwood, holly, hemlock, rhododendron, false cypress, or bayberry.

You may have to adapt the garden a little to include larger woody plants amid smaller herbs. Woody plants usually win if they compete for rooting space with smaller herbs. It's your job, as designer, to plan ahead and prevent conflicts. When underplanting trees with herbs, prepare the soil well and water and fertilize extra if necessary. When putting herbs under mature shade trees, look for pockets of soil up near the trunk, where little root activity occurs. If you have a hedge around your herb garden, leave an access path between the shrubs and the herb garden; this also allows for root clearance.

HARDSCAPE & ACCESSORIES

Most herbs, though beautiful and useful, change over time, leaving the garden in need of some stability. Unchanging elements such as walks, retaining walls, fences, and accessories help to define the garden, give it enduring beauty, and create structure year in and year out. These permanent, nonliving landscape elements are called "hardscape."

Here's how you can improve your garden's appearance and usefulness with hardscape. Begin by trying to blend whatever you build with the existing structures in the rest of the landscape. Pick one or two kinds of construction materials, preferably kinds that are used elsewhere around the yard, and stick with them. For example, if you already have a brick house, make brick walks in your herb garden. If you already have a flagstone walk, make stone walls to raise or surround your herb garden. If your house is formal, use rectangular stones; informal houses and gardens fit well with paths made of irregularly shaped flagstone.

Coordinate the colors of the building materials with your favorite herbs. Blend pink or red brick with pink-flowered roses and thymes, or the pink highlights on the foliage of 'Tricolor' sage. Use light-colored stone with white-flowered rosemary, or white-variegated pineapple mint. But use darker-colored stone, pebbles, or bricks to show off silver foliage such as silver sage, 'Himalayan Silver' spearmint, and gray santolina.

Practical Uses of Hardscape

Build structures for beauty, easy access, and site improvement. Here are some possibilities.

Retaining Walls for Raised Beds. If your garden area is low, has shallow soil, or is poorly drained, you can raise the bed with timbers, boards, stones, or a brick retaining wall. The raised areas of the bed will drain better, plus your garden will take on a more interesting structure. You can complete the raised garden with softscape; let catmint or winter savory cascade over the wall or let thyme grow in the cracks between rocks or bricks.

© Rosalind Creasy

Fine bark chips cover a winding pathway through a garden of clary sage, common sage, oregano, garlic chives, and thymes.

Access Walks. If your garden is over 5 feet wide, you probably tramp through it (mashing the soil and dirtying your shoes) whenever you walk through to gather herbs for dinner. Avoid both problems by putting one or more access paths in the garden. Make a natural looking path of bark mulch or gravel over some weed-suppressing landscape fabric. Or add stepping stones or build a paved stone or brick walk. Brick walks, especially those made of old bricks, are attractive in most herb gardens. Lay out access paths or walks so they create interesting patterns of their own. Use straight paths to divide a square garden into four equal squares or a circle into wedges. In a freeform bed, use a gently curving or winding path to divide the garden into two or three graceful shapes.

Enclosures. Does the herb garden seem to get lost in the expanse of your yard? Or do neighborhood kids and dogs regularly romp through it? For reasons of security or to separate the garden visually into its own unique space, you may want to surround it with a fence or a wall. (A hedge can also do the job.)

For a merely symbolic enclosure, you can install rustic split-rail fences, wattle fences (woven twigs or branches), or open trellises covered with vines. Or make low brick or stone walls, if you use those materials elsewhere in your yard.

For more substantial fencing, try traditional picket fences. Fortunately, we don't need 8-foot-tall stockade fences to keep out wolves and wandering packs of outlaws anymore. Tall enclosures make a small yard seem even smaller and create extra shade, which can limit the number of herbs you can grow.

What about Accessories?

Accessories are great in a garden; they add a hint of personality, an aura of history, the excitement of contemporary times, or the luster of romance. But you must pick accessories carefully so they contribute to the overall design without cluttering it up.

Try to choose items appropriate to the period you are representing in your design, and to the other colors and materials used. For instance, a Victorian stone urn planted with cascading 'Apple' scented geraniums

© Karen Bussolini / Positive Images

A traditional collection of mints, santolina, basils, and thymes is well protected by a surrounding picket fence.

Building Your Own Hardscape Features

If you're handy around the house, you can easily build garden structures yourself and save labor expenses. Small projects are fairly easy if you have time, patience, and enthusiasm. Check out a couple of books on the subject from the library and use quality materials.

I've made low, dry, stone retaining walls by building layers of flat stones up to about a foot high. And I've put in a brick walk by digging a shallow path, smoothing level sand in the bottom, laying the brick in a basketweave pattern, and filling in the cracks.

Big projects, such as a tall wall, large patio, or terrace on a steep hillside, may require a professional. For stone, brick, or wood work, you can use specialized stone masons, bricklayers, or carpenters. You also can hire landscape contractors, who usually do a wide range of landscape jobs. However, some might do a better job with a particular kind of material; ask around and look at their portfolio of previous jobs to confirm their qualifications.

Here's how to make a simple brick walk.

1 Prepare the area for a brick walk. Dig deep enough to remove sod and weeds in the area. With stakes and twine, mark the boundaries. Rake the surface level and remove stones.

Scrape the ground level, tamp it down firmly, and spread several inches of sand on top. Scrape it smooth again.

Lay bricks in the pattern of your choice, allowing space between bricks for mortar. Use a board the width of your walkway to kneel on as you work your way down.

2 For mortar, mix 3 parts sand and 1 part cement with enough water to make a fairly smooth mixture. Wet the pavement, then pour the mortar mixture on top of it. With a yard broom, brush the mortar into the joints. Do a small area at a time, and hose the bricks clean as you go, but work rapidly before the mortar hardens.

An alternative to using mortar is to lay the bricks right against each other and sweep sand into the gaps when you have finished.

Plantings along the path will quickly fill out, and your brick path will look like it always belonged there.

would be ideal in a bright tapestry garden combining annual flowers and herbs. An Elizabethan sundial might bring out the best in a knot garden. A formal herb garden could be enhanced by a marble statue. Skeps, old-fashioned domed beehives made of straw, are often used as ornaments in traditional herb gardens. A naturalistic garden might be even more comfortable with a rustic wooden bench. A contemporary garden could be highlighted by white molded plastic chairs. Birdbaths are welcome additions to any garden.

Kellie O'Brien, a designer with English Gardens, Ltd., uses a morning glory–covered antique water pump as a garden accent. It is next to a miniature concrete water trough 2 feet long and 1½ feet wide. The trough is planted with thyme and other miniature plants that otherwise might get lost in the garden. Troughs work well as accents within a larger garden, serving as miniature container gardens. They also provide the hot and dry conditions that many Mediterranean herbs like. Hand-hewn stone troughs are durable but hard to find. It's easier to find or make cement troughs.

© Karen Bussolini / Positive Images

Choose accessories that contribute to the overall design of your herb garden.

You can find garden accessories in a variety of places. Start at a local garden center. If their selection is limited, check out stone or cast-cement suppliers, stone cutters, landscapers, potters, sculptors, and woodworkers; craft shows, flea markets, antique dealers, and want ads. Or browse through mail-order catalogues. Many companies specialize in benches, stone lanterns, trellises, rose arbors, and similar specialties, which they would be happy to ship to you (though shipping can be expensive).

A POTPOURRI OF GARDEN DESIGNS

Take a moment to think about what kind of herb garden design would work best for you. If you've got an older home, you may want to use a design from history. If you have a small condominium courtyard, you could try an old-fashioned cottage garden. Or you might enjoy cultivating low-growing and creeping herbs in a rock garden, or planting especially curious and aromatic herbs in a garden designed to appeal to children.

You'll find numerous herb garden ideas here to help you, plus suggestions on how to incorporate herbs into the rest of your landscape. Browse through them carefully to find one that appeals to you and is appropriate for your yard and style of architecture. Remember, if you're limited in time or space, every portion of the garden needs to pull its own weight. So weed out any herbs or features that you don't feel are essential.

An Informal, Kidney-Shaped Garden. Make an island bed in a sunny corner of your yard. It should be about twice as long as wide and feature large sweeping curves. Use one kind of edging plant along the concave curve and a different edging plant along the convex curve to define the garden and give it a little

A small, Kidney-Shaped Herb Garden in a corner of your yard is inviting to the eye.

Knot Gardens take advantage of different kinds, colors, and textures of herb foliage. The top drawing shows the basic knot; below, a square and circle are added for a more complex design.

all the beautiful flowers we grow today. Instead of flowers, knot gardens took advantage of the many kinds, colors, and textures of herbal foliage, interwoven into fanciful designs.

Choose herbs for the knots whose textures and growth habits are similar enough so one won't overpower the other. But the colors, textures, and growth habits shouldn't be exactly the same in order to give the knot some contrast in form.

You can start with a simple knot made of two interlinking circles, triangles, or squares, each of which uses a different kind of herb. Make sure you get the lines straight and the circles round before you plant your knot garden. To get the layout right, first draw the pattern on the prepared soil with a hoe or sprinkle of lime. Stretch a rope between two stakes to lay out straight lines. Lay out circles by putting a stake in the center of the circle and attaching a rope half as long as the diameter of the circle. Circle it around the stake to mark the circle perimeter. To find the center of the garden, put a stake in each corner. Stretch a string between opposite stakes; they'll cross in the middle.

To create the appearance of solid or continuous lines or groups, space herbs close enough so they will grow into each other. As a general rule, space perennial herbs such as teucrium, lavender, gray or green santolina, and 'Silver Carpet' lamb's ears about 8 inches apart. Space annuals such as basil, marigold, nasturtium, parsley, and perilla about 5 inches apart.

It's important to choose herbs whose textures and growth habits are similar so they won't overpower each other. This knot garden shows how massing herbs closely can allow them to grow into planned configurations.

© Liz Ball, Photo/Nats

Knot Gardening in a Container

Holly Shimizu, assistant director of the U.S. Botanic Garden, likes to make miniature knot gardens in containers for display on the Botanic Garden terrace.

One of her knot designs features a figure eight of thyme with chamomile in each corner and two potted rosemary topiaries in the openings of the "eight." These plants need shearing about once every three weeks to keep them shapely.

Another favorite combines dwarf purple basil and dwarf curry plant, which look great together and only need clipping once or twice a season. "The basil has a more rounded, full, and billowy shape, while the curry plant is stiffer. This kind of variety of form and texture adds to the beauty of the knot," adds Shimizu.

For a more formal knot, Shimizu recommends blending two upright varieties of thyme, such as a narrow-leaved, gray variety and a rounder-leaved, green variety. Keep them pruned sharply into a low, stiff hedge.

Shimizu uses wooden containers 2½ feet wide by 5 feet long. The containers are easy to maintain; filled with a specially blended soil, they are free of weed seeds and drain well, which limits problems with diseases. But they may need daily watering in hot weather and require treatment with water-soluble fertilizer (such as a blend of fish emulsion and seaweed) every 2 weeks.

Shimizu mixes her own soil with one part peat-based growing mix, one part compost, and one part peat moss. She blends this with equal parts of good loamy topsoil to produce a soil with some substance.

Because it's not practical to keep the knots during the winter at the U.S. Botanic Garden, Shimizu discards the plants at the end of the season and replants new knot gardens when she needs them again. But you can keep your knot garden going year after year, she says. Start with hardy herbs and cover the container during winter to keep the soil from freezing through. Or move it to a cool spot indoors, keeping the soil slightly moist.

(Adapted from an article by Holly Shimizu, *Herb Companion*, 1991, vol. 3, no. 4.)

Herbal Landscaping Beds

You can bring herbs out of the herb garden and into the landscape. Let them edge a foundation planting, bring color or fragrance to a perennial garden, or provide contrast to a bed of annual flowers. Here are some ideas that will make your landscape more beautiful and productive.

Spice up your flower garden with the unique form, color, fragrance, and texture of herbs. Use low, emerald green mounds of bush basil in the foreground of a flower bed. Use dill to provide upright accents in a mass of bedding annuals. Blend clumps of blue-flowered lavender into a bed of pink petunias. Combine fragrant 'Lemon Gem' marigolds with upright blue salvia. Blend red chile peppers with red geraniums and yellow zinnias. Use 'Moonbeam' coreopsis against a backdrop of bronze fennel. Other good herbs for flower gardens include chives, artemisias, rue, sages, and yarrow.

If you get tired of mowing and trimming grass beneath trees, under-plant them with a herbal ground cover such as lady's mantle, English

Herbal Lawns

Historical herb garden designs are as enjoyable now as in the past. For example, the herbal lawn is again becoming fashionable, although for a different purpose and in a different form.

Lawns once used fragrant, low-growing herbs such as Roman chamomile to produce a scented turf where lords and ladies could sit and enjoy the soft aromas that arose around trailing skirts and ruffled petticoats. It's a romantic thought, but one that hardly meets today's notions of what a lawn should be.

Modern herbal lawns are a rebellion against sterile, chemically treated contemporary lawns. Their owners avoid herbicides and encourage herbs to grow and spread amid the grass. For example, my yard has plenty of fragrant ground ivy, smaller pussytoes (*Antennaria neglecta*) with woolly white flowers for drying, wild strawberries, and yarrow, which is fragrant and also has flowers for drying. Your yard might feature these or other herbs, such as clover, violets, chamomile, English pennyroyal, and mother-of-thyme. The herbs you choose should be low growing or tolerant of mowing, and they should spread fairly quickly.

To add herbs to your yard, dig out patches of turf, removing it roots and all. Then fill the barren spots with good topsoil and plant large nursery-grown herbs or herb divisions. Water well until the herbs begin to grow, but fertilize minimally so nearby grasses won't become too aggressive.

pennyroyal, or sweet woodruff. Remember, these shade-tolerant herbs will grow better under trees with deep root systems, such as oaks, ashes, lindens, and honey locusts. They often struggle under shallow-rooted trees such as catalpas, maples, sweet gums, willows, and poplars.

Herbs can add a wonderful touch to your foundation plantings. Slip in a few taller herbs such as fennel, angelica, or lovage on either side of your front door or by the edges of the house. Use smaller herbs in large masses for edging or clustering near evergreens that need brightening up. And keep in mind that durable herbs such as mint, lovage, and angelica can hold their own in a naturalized garden or meadow planting.

PRACTICAL ASPECTS OF GARDEN DESIGN

While you are thinking about the best way to design your garden, consider how your design can simplify ongoing maintenance and enhance enjoyment of the garden. If you can incorporate a few of the following conveniences, you'll save yourself time and trouble in years to come.

(Opposite) Pebbled stepping stones contrast handsomely with this herbal lawn of creeping thyme (*Thymus praecox articus*).

Photo: © Thomas E. Eltzroth

To Label or Not to Label

Labels make it easy for you to remember what you've planted and where it is. But many white, yellow, and green plastic labels are intrusive as well as temporary. They're easy to break or push out of the soil and lose. Sometimes even if you don't lose the label itself, the so-called permanent ink on it fades in only a few months, leaving you without a clue as to which herb is which. There are other options — none of which is ideal. Wooden tags are slightly more durable and less obtrusive than plastic, but the writing fades faster. Terra-cotta labels, although handsome and earthy, are also temporary. They can shatter during cold winter months. Other ornmental carved or crafted name tags, although handsome, are usually

© Kevin Kennefick

Metal nameplates help you identify what you have planted.

rather generic. They usually don't include the species and variety names — and that's the part of the name that's hard to remember.

The most practical option, although far from beautiful, is a metal nameplate on foot-long stakes that you can push into the ground. The plates are soft, so when you write on them with a hard ballpoint pen, you leave an indentation. When the ink fades, you'll still be able to see the imprint of the name. You can also find soft aluminum tags that you can wire fairly unobtrusively onto an interior branch of a woody herb.

If you don't like labels, your other option is to keep track of your plants on a garden map that you update as necessary. This way you don't have to scatter silver or white labels around the garden. But you will need to make a point of storing the map where it'll be easy to find and update regularly — at least every spring and fall. If you neglect it for a year, you may forget the names and locations of new acquisitions.

Minimizing Maintenance

Half the fun of having an herb garden is getting out there to take care of it. You can lounge in the sun, smell the mints you've just cut, examine the soft fuzz on the leaf of a rose geranium, and watch your parsley plants swell. But herb gardening should not be time consuming. Organize your garden so maintenance remains light and fun; then it'll never be a chore.

To minimize maintenance, use a little judgment when you're planning. Referring to some herb books may give you grand ideas that are hard to keep up. Let's face it. Most of us no longer devote our entire day to tending plants, and we don't have large staffs to keep our herb gardens neat and trim. Instead, we have to rely on time- and trouble-saving devices, and careful planning, using some of the ideas that follow.

- Don't put large or aggressive plants such as mints and 'Silver King' artemisia in small spaces. These plants are hard on neighboring herbs. They crowd them, grow through them, or cover them over with foliage and roots. No matter what kind of takeover plan aggressive herbs employ, their wandering ways make it hard to keep the garden tidy and to keep neighboring plants separate and healthy. It's even harder to

PART THREE

Seasons
in the
Herb Garden

CHAPTER 6

SPRING IN THE HERB GARDEN

Perennials awake in spring, and their leaves fill out with soft new growth. Hardy, fast-growing annuals such as arugula and cilantro emerge from seeds after the fickle weather of spring passes. Slower-growing herb seedlings such as parsley need a head start indoors under lights or in a greenhouse. And many perennials are ripe for making root cuttings, dividing, or layering.

Busy spring, a time of gentle warmth and new beginnings, arrives at different times from place to place and year to year. In the North, as in my neighborhood in Cleveland, Ohio, it may come in April but is more likely to keep us waiting until May. Spring frosts generally are over by Memorial Day -- although sometimes they finish up a little earlier and occasionally come a little later.

In warmer climates, gentle springlike weather may arrive as early as February. It could continue for months before summery heat takes over. Don't run to the calender to see when spring officially starts. Instead, think of spring as the time when the weather becomes mild and you can start gardening again.

EARLY SPRING: GETTING STARTED

Because early spring is often cold or wet, it becomes a great time to tackle indoor gardening tasks. You also can tend to pruning, weeding, and cleaning out the garden beds. Then when the pleasant

~

(Opposite page)

French sorrel, pansies, and chives are among the first signs of spring.

~

Photo: © David Cavagnaro

When Can You Expect Spring?

In Cleveland the spring gardening season usually begins 4 to 6 weeks before the average last spring frost date. Find your location on the map below to determine the average last spring frost date in your area. Then ask your Cooperative Extension agent when you can plant cool-weather hardy herbs in your area.

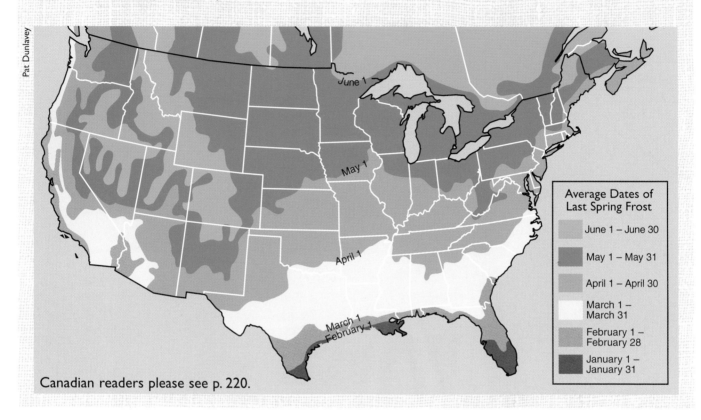

Pat Dunlavey

Average Dates of Last Spring Frost

June 1 – June 30
May 1 – May 31
April 1 – April 30
March 1 – March 31
February 1 – February 28
January 1 – January 31

Canadian readers please see p. 220.

warmth, swollen flower buds, and migrating birds actually arrive, you'll be ready to prepare and plant the garden.

Starting Plants from Seeds

Think about what you would like to grow: Decide if you want a bed full of basil — some for you, some more for frozen pesto, still more for giving dried to friends or selling fresh to nearby restaurants or farm stands. Or grow specialty herbs not usually available, such as gourmet varieties of thyme that will awe and amaze your gardening friends and expand your herb collection. Propagate a few plants of everything you need; it will be a fraction of the cost of buying plants at a nursery. (However, to propagate from other plants — rather than seed — you need to buy or have access to the plant you are going to propagate from.)

Fortunately, propagating herbs is easy — anyone can do it. All you have to do is find the right technique. If you're willing to take the time to start your own seeds, the sky is the limit. You can choose from scores of herb species.

Plants such as basil and dill are a snap to start from seed. But seedlings of perennials such as rosemary may seem to take forever to reach good size and even then may not be as good as their parents. You're better off cloning these herbs by vegetative propagation. You can divide a large plant into sections. Or if you want a dozen or more plants of a particular herb, you can take cuttings — a common nursery propagation procedure. Here are some propagation methods for you to try.

Starting Seeds Indoors

To give herbs a jump on the growing season, you can start most herb seeds indoors. (Once you work out a system, it is easy.) Soaking seeds for

Which Plants to Grow from Seeds

Some herbs grow well from seeds, fulfilling your every expectation. And some are great to let self-sow and give you another generation of plants, trouble-free. But other herbs don't produce seed or don't grow into top-quality plants from seeds. They're better propagated vegetatively, by cuttings or division.

Herbs that seldom produce seeds:
French tarragon, lemon verbena, and garlic.

Herbs that grow reliably from seeds:
Anise, anise hyssop, basils (including named cultivars such as 'Opal' and 'Lemon'), bee balm, borage, salad burnet, catnip, German chamomile, chives, garlic chives, cresses, dill (including named cultivars such as

'Fernleaf'), fennel, hyssop, English lavender, spike lavender, woolly lavender, a few specific lavender cultivars such as 'Lavender Lady' and 'Hidcote Blue', lemon balm, lovage, sweet marjoram, onions, oregano, parsley, pennyroyal, chile peppers, perilla, rosemary, sage, sorrel, summer savory, sweet Annie artemisia, thyme de Provence, and valerian.

Herbs that show considerable variation:
Most cultivars (as opposed to species) of many herbs, including bee balm, lavender (except those mentioned above), mint, oregano, rosemary, sage, thyme, yarrow, and more show considerable variation if started from seed. These are all propagated vegetatively by, making cuttings, layering, or dividing.

©Kevin Kennefick

Presprout seeds that are known to be slow to sprout by placing them between damp paper towels and putting them into a zip-sealing bag. Check to see if they have sprouted after a few days, but don't let them sit in dampness too much longer — they may rot.

plants them, and starts them growing. Angelica and sweet cicely also benefit if you refrigerate the seeds to keep them viable and provide a winterlike cold that encourages sprouting once you return the seeds to a warm place.

You also can stratify slow-germinating perennial seeds by sowing the seeds in small trays. First keep them warm and moist, then freeze them in a plastic bag for 2 weeks. Give them another warm period and more freezing again if necessary. This simulates the natural germination requirements of herbs with northern homelands.

Some herbs, such as yarrow and others with very fine seeds, need light to germinate. Simply press them into moist growing mix and cover the top with clear plastic.

If you are going to undertake starting seeds indoors, you will need to consider the raw materials needed. If you have all the ingredients, your results should be not only successful but extremely satisfying.

Soil. When starting seeds indoors, use sterile, lightweight seed-starting mix. Commercial seed-starting mixes are usually a blend of vermiculite and finely ground sphagnum moss. A sterile growing mix is important to prevent most disease problems common to young seedlings. But if it dries out, it's hard to rewet. So before planting, wet the mix down well until it's as wet as a wrung-out sponge (which takes more water than you might expect).

Sow the seeds according to the package directions. Then keep the growing mix constantly moist by bottom-watering (submerging the bottom of the pot briefly in water) or gently sprinkling the surface. Keeping a greenhouselike cover of clear plastic over the container of seedlings will help keep the mix from drying out.

Containers. If you reuse containers for seeds, be sure to sterilize them first. Disinfect plastic containers by scrubbing them with a solution of 1 part bleach in 10 parts water. Rinse well before preparing to plant.

If you want to grow a lot of plants, save space (initially), and don't mind transplanting the seedlings into larger pots when they get over-crowded, you can start seedlings in a large, rectangular flat. I like to line out seeds in rows, growing plants with similar germinating times together so I can transplant the entire flat at the same time. I label each row with a short tag and cover the flat with clear plastic wrap.

Another option is to start seedlings in plug trays, which are the same size as a standard nursery flat but full of thimble-sized pockets for easy transplanting. If you can't find plug trays locally, you can order them from mail-order garden suppliers.

You can also plant herb seeds directly into larger 3- or 4-inch pots, plastic six-packs (like those you see used for bedding annuals), or plastic cups (which are prone to tipping over but inexpensive and easy to find). Just be sure to perforate containers at the bottom so excess water can drain out. Planting in larger pots takes up more space initially but saves you from having to transplant into larger pots before you can set the seedlings out.

You can start plants with sensitive roots (such as dill) in peat pots so you can plant the seedlings, pot and all, when the time is right. Unfortunately, peat-based containers dry out faster than a plastic pot, so you'll have to check their moistness daily to keep the seedlings from wilting. Also be aware that peat pots may not degrade completely after you plant them. Tear off the upper rim so it doesn't dry out if not totally submerged after planting. I also try to break up the walls and bottom gently — without disturbing the roots — just to ensure that the roots can escape. (I once grew a very large cockscomb, only to find after pulling it up that the roots had never left the peat pot.)

Water. Keep the growing mix moist but not wet. Use slightly warm water rather than shockingly cold water. Use a fine mist sprayer to avoid dislodging young seedlings or bottom-water by submerging the growing container in a shallow container of water. Some seedlings with roots that are prone to rot, such as lavender or basil, do best if you let the soil dry out slightly between waterings. Others such as chile peppers do best if kept evenly moist.

Avoid softened water, which can be salty and burn seedling roots. And if you're having trouble growing pH-sensitive herbs such as lavender, check if your water is especially acidic or alkaline, which might be causing problems. (See pp. 36–37.)

One method for watering seedlings is bottom-watering. Place six-packs in a tray of water and let them stand long enough to soak up the moisture they need.

Light. All seedlings need light to grow into stocky and healthy plants. Unfortunately, sunlight that comes through a window is rarely consistent or bright enough. If the window is shaded part of the day or the weather is cloudy for a couple days, the seedlings can stretch up scrawny and limp as they search for the sun. Weak plants such as these seldom do well outdoors.

A good alternative to the window is a fluorescent light garden. Simply hang a shop light fixture (which has two tubes, each 4 feet long) over the seedlings; put it as close as you can without touching the plants. Then set the lights on a timer so they shine 14 to 16 hours a day and turn off and on automatically. For extra brilliance, use new fluorescent tubes (after a few seasons, tubes produce much less light) and surround the light-garden area with shiny aluminum foil to reflect the brightness toward the seedlings.

Fertilizer. Some soil mixes come complete with a small amount of fertilizer, which gives the seedlings a slight boost when they are very young. Ordinarily, you wouldn't add much more or it would damage the roots or they may begin to grow too rapidly and become scrawny. But if you grow seedlings for weeks on end in the same pot, or if you keep them in a container outdoors through part of the summer, you'll need to fertilize. Use a balanced organic fertilizer diluted ¼ or ½ strength, and apply every 2 to 4 weeks.

TAKING CUTTINGS

You can grow new plants from pieces of stems or roots of many herbs, which are called "cuttings." Cuttings have several advantages. They almost always grow into little clones of the parent plant (so you'll know what you're getting right from the start). By late spring you can use stem cuttings — sections of young stems supplied with a few leaves — which will grow new roots along the lower part of the stem. Or in mid-spring you can use root cuttings, which sprout roots from downward facing buds and shoots from upward facing buds.

Easy Rooting in Plastic Bags

You can root cuttings in anything: water, straight sand, peat mixes, vermiculite, and perlite. But Brian Holley, director of Cleveland Botanical Garden, recommends a simple alternative. Stick cuttings in peat-based mixes in a clear plastic bag. This will keep the cuttings in a protected humid area and eliminate messy soil spills. Keep the cutting bag in indirect light until the cuttings begin to root.

Plants that send out runners (such as apple mint) are easy to propagate from root cuttings. Clean your knife and cutting surface with a solution of bleach in water (1:10). Cut a runner into sections several inches long.

Put root cuttings in moist, sterile grower's mix in clean containers, and place them in a bright location.

© Kevin Kennefick

©Kevin Kennefick

Use the same set-up for starting cuttings as you would for starting seeds. Grow them in flats, plug trays, or other containers in a bright location as detailed for seeds. Use a porous, fast-draining mix of peat and perlite or sand. Some growers prefer a 50:50 blend of vermiculite and perlite. Sometimes you can even root stem cuttings of herbs such as mints, bee balm, and pineapple sage in jars of water on the windowsill. Remove the leaves below the waterline and change the water daily to discourage rotting.

Stem Cuttings

Begin with a section of healthy, flowerless stem that has been growing steadily for the past month or two. (Indoor plants are good for stem cuttings in the spring, but for outdoor plants you'll have to wait until summer.) Side shoots coming off the main stem are often ideal. The tissue should be firm enough that you can't pinch it off easily.

Remove the cutting with pruning shears scrubbed with a solution of 1 part bleach to 10 parts water. Make a slanting cut just below the lowest set of leaves (a slanted cut exposes more layers of tissue to draw up water and nutrients while roots are forming). If you are cutting a shoot into several

Scented geraniums are particularly easy to start from stem cuttings. As with root cuttings, always use utensils that have been cleaned in a solution of bleach in water (1:10).

Remove lower leaves that would sit on or below the surface of the soil. Put stem cuttings in moist, sterile grower's mix in clean containers, and place them in a bright location.

pieces, make the cut at the top horizontal so you can tell which way is up. If you have problems with scented geranium cuttings rotting instead of rooting, let them sit out to cure overnight before sticking them in planting mix.

Remove the leaves on the lower portion of the cutting, leaving only naked stem. Along the naked stem are the primary places that new roots will form. Leave at least one or preferably two sets of leaves at the top of the cutting. You can treat the lower portion of the stem with rooting hormones if you like, but it's not always necessary. Rooting hormones are natural root-stimulating compounds put in an easy-to-use powder that will cling to the cutting.

To plant cuttings, make a hole in moist potting mix, insert the leafless base of the cutting, and press the soil firmly around it. Some herb cuttings such as basil are prone to wilting. Cover their container with clear plastic, propped up above the herb foliage to keep the air damp but the foliage dry. Providing bottom heat with a heating cable may speed root development. The cuttings will be ready to transplant when they start to grow or when you tug on them gently and they have enough roots to resist.

Suggestions for Stem Cuttings

Artemisia	Oregano
Bee balm	Pineapple sage
Lavender	Rosemary
Lemon verbena	Scented geraniums
Mint	Thyme

HARDENING OFF

When your seedlings or cuttings have reached a reasonable size for transplanting, you need to get them ready to face the rigors of life outdoors before setting them free in the soil. Drying wind, pelting rain, freezing frost, and burning sun can all damage tender young leaves and stems that have come directly from a protected environment indoors. They will need to be hardened off.

When the weather outdoors is mild, move the young plants out for several hours and then return them indoors or to another sheltered location. Increase their exposure to the elements daily, taking care they don't wilt, freeze, or sunburn from overexposure. Within a week or so, your young plants will be ready to go.

Note: You don't need to harden off hardy divisions or layered plantlets that are already accustomed to growing outdoors.

When Is Your Soil Ready to Work?

You'll know a good deal about how early you can get into your garden once you learn what kind of soil you have (see pp. 32–33, chapter 4). Sandy soils warm up and dry out fast and can be ready to work at the first dawning of spring. Clay soils, on the other hand, stay sticky, cold, and damp well into spring — delaying your access date as much as a month or more after that of a sandy soil.

Why wait? If you tread, shovel, or till in soils before they are dry enough, you clump the now-separate soil particles together — turning clay soils into brick by summertime. Take my word for it — it'll happen!

You can double-check the wetness or readiness of the soil with a simple squeeze test before you start shoveling or tilling. Squeeze a handful of soil into a ball. If you can break the ball up easily with a light tap of your finger, then it is ready to be worked. If the ball of soil clings in a sodden mass, wait a few days and check it again.

On the other hand, if the soil is totally parched, working it will raise a lot of dust and disrupt the underground soil life. So if the soil won't cling into a ball, wet it down well and let it sit a day before digging in it.

STARTING SEEDS OUTDOORS

Don't rush spring planting outdoors. Let the garden soil dry enough to tolerate foot traffic. And wait until temperatures are right for planting or seeding.

The easiest way to deal with seeds is to sow them directly in the soil. This works best with herbs such as basil, dill, mustard, and cilantro that have fairly large seeds and that grow quickly. Plant twice as many seeds as you need. If the temperature, moisture, and soil are right, many will come up; if they all sprout, you can pull every other one out or move them elsewhere.

Sowing Seeds Outdoors

1. Prepare the soil carefully before direct-sowing. You need a fine, light soil that lets seedlings emerge easily.

2. Plant seeds when soil temperatures are right for them. Cool-season herbs (e.g., arugula) favor cool soil and warm-season herbs prefer warm soil.

3. Check directions on the seed packet for depth and spacing.

4. Plant herbs in straight or double rows for edgings or for cutting in a vegetable garden. Or thinly sprinkle quick-growing annuals such as mustard,

Buying Plants

There may be occasions when you have to buy plants, and you need to know how to choose the best quality. If you want particular species and cultivars, plant-shopping can get a little complicated. It's important to buy plants from a reputable nursery. Start locally so you can see the herbs to be sure they are what you want. Rub your fingers across the leaves and smell the aroma that clings to your fingers.

If you can't find a specific species or cultivar, ask. The nursery may call it by a different name. You also can get sound advice from mail-order herb specialists, which are good places to try if you can't find what you want locally. Once you find the herbs you need, take note of where you bought them so you'll know where to go for replacements in the future.

Ideally, you should buy from someone who doesn't mind telling you how the plants were propagated. Check whether herbs such as mint and thyme were grown vegetatively or from seed (which can produce variable results).

(Top Left) To sow seeds in a straight row after the soil has been prepared, first mark the row with string, and make a trench the depth the seed should be planted according to the instructions on the seed packet.

(Bottom Left) To sow seeds over a wide bed after the soil has been prepared, mark the wide area you wish to cover, and spread seed generously over that area. Afterwards you can gently pull a rake over the area to cover the seeds or sift good topsoil over the area to cover the seeds.

(Top Right) For interesting masses of herbs in your garden, try sowing seeds in geometric patterns. Here a square area was divided and four smaller areas were planted with different herbs.

Pruning When Planting

Some older books have recommended pruning woody plants before planting them. But if you buy a thriving balled or container-grown plant, this is not necessary. In fact, the branch tips (which would be lost if you pruned) supply hormones that encourage faster root growth. So leave the branches all there to photosynthesize and keep the roots stretching.

Likewise, plant roots seldom need pruning before planting. But there are a few exceptions. If you pull the plant out of its pot and find roots that are tangled or matted inside the pot, you can prune them a little to break them free. You should also remove any damaged or diseased roots that you find on new plants and divisions.

arugula, dill, and basil across wide beds. Thin the young plants to use in salads or for seasonings, leaving the remaining herbs enough room to mature.

5. Label the seeded area well so you know which plants are your herbs.

6. Keep the seeded area moist. If the weather is dry, sprinkle gently with a fine mist so you don't wash smaller seeds away.

In ornamental gardens, sow herb seeds so that you can thin them to make groups of three plants in a triangle, five in a pentagon, or a larger group of seven, nine, or more for natural-looking clumps or drifts. You might space the seeds closer than necessary so you'll have extra seedlings to fill in anywhere a required plant fails. You can also move young seedlings of most plants to a new location if necessary. But don't bother taprooted herbs such as dill, Florence fennel, and caraway. They may die from root disturbance.

PRUNING

Early spring — before plants break out of dormancy — is a great time to prune woody plants that give structure to your herb garden. Leafless deciduous trees and shrubs give you a clear view of their branching framework, so you can easily decide which areas are overcrowded and need a little thinning to develop a more balanced or graceful shape. Thin back lanky or aged branches to the base or to a side shoot that is growing toward an open area of the plant. Also be sure to trim out any dead or diseased wood.

Low-growing woody herbs benefit from spring pruning, removing old growth. Once your herbs start growing again in spring, you can begin to trim up any that have developed brittle, dead twigs during the winter.

Bushy herbs, such as santolina, can be trimmed easily with hedge shears.

Dead twigs will be brown, easy to snap off, and unable to resprout. But lavender may only *appear* to be dead because it is so slow to start growing. Prune it last when you're sure the barren twigs are really dead. You can shape and prune sheared plants such as winter savory, gray santolina, and hyssop with grass or hedge shears. But use pruning shears to remove individual dead sprigs on herbs such as rosemary and lavender where you want a more natural shape.

FROST BEATERS

Even though you've waited until the safe planting time, late, unexpected frost may threaten. Then rather than crossing your fingers and hoping for the best, protect vulnerable plants. Here's a rundown of the available options.

Floating Row Covers. You can cover plants for weeks on end with these lightweight, clothlike covers. They allow light and moisture to pass through and can keep plants several degrees warmer than the air temperature.

Jumpy Plants

Soil that alternatively freezes and thaws during winter will expand and contract (a process called "frost heaving"), sometimes tossing out clumps of roots like lava from a volcano. This is most likely to affect shallow-rooted or newly planted herbs, so don't be surprised if you see them protruding out of the soil early in spring.

Fortunately, frost heaving is easy to fix. Simply reset the root ball at the original level and press it firmly into place. Make a note for next year to mulch the soil after it freezes in winter so it will stay frozen and won't be heaving plants around.

Fabric. Wrap up plants temporarily on a frosty night with burlap or some other kind of material that will keep the frost off the plants. Be sure to remove the fabric in the morning so the plants can get light and air.

Plastic. Make a plastic dome over plants for a frosty nights. For extended cool-season growing, enclose low-growing herbs in a clear plastic tunnel — a miniature replica of an unheated greenhouse. Make a tunnel of this sort by stretching a sheet of clear plastic over croquet-wicket-like arches of wire. Leave the tunnel ends loose so air can circulate through during the day. As the weather warms up later in spring, you may have to cut flaps in the sides of the plastic so plants won't overheat.

Cloche or Old Soda Bottle. You can cover individual small plants with the translucent top of a two-liter soda bottle. Cut off the bottom and push the cut end down into the soil. You also can buy similar plastic tunnels that surround single plants and trap heat around them. But don't be surprised if either kind of cloche takes to the air on a windy day; they aren't very heavy or stable.

Wall O'Water. This product is a teepee of water-holding tubes that will enclose a single plant. The water heats up during the day and helps keep

© Gay Bumgarner, Photo/Nats

Plastic tentlike covers are one means of protecting tender herbs during cold nights.

the plant warm and insulated at night. Wall O'Waters are a little tricky to set up but you can use them for several weeks. Just check inside the walls occasionally to be sure the plant has enough water and fresh air to grow well.

Buckets or Bushel Baskets. A fast way to protect a group of herbs on a cold night is to cover them with a bucket or bushel basket — even an inverted plant pot. Remove the cover when the weather warms up the next day.

Now the rush of early spring is almost over. Perennials are starting to come up full force, and it's time to set nursery plants in the garden.

PLANTING TIME

Spring is a time for new starts, new gardens, and planting. Resolve to get new herbs safely into the ground after carefully planning your design and preparing your soil. When your new plants are hardened off, the soil is fairly dry, and the weather is sufficiently mild, you can lay out your herb beds.

Begin by raking the soil into a flat or mounded bed, depending on the look you want. Then lay out all the herbs you've collected to see if they look as good together as you imagined. Outline the positions of herb edgings and groups with a flexible rubber hose, a rope, a trickle of white limestone, or a string stretched between two stakes. (When you need access inside the bed, lay down a board to walk on so you won't compact the soil with your footsteps.) Then set the plants in their allotted space and stand back to take a critical look at the results. Fine-tune the spacing and organization, if necessary. When you feel comfortable with the layout, go ahead and plant.

Assuming you've prepared the entire garden bed ahead of time, you shouldn't add soil amendments to individual planting sites. (In fact, this could prevent the root system from stretching beyond the amended area into the soil.) Make a hole as deep as the root ball — or slightly deeper because recently rototilled soil will sink over the next couple of months . Fill it with water. Pop the plants out of their pots. If the plants are in peat pots, peel off

© Kevin Kennefick

© Kevin Kennefick

(Left) Before you set your herbs in the ground, consider the placement. Ground limestone can be used to mark off areas.

(Right) Dig a hole as deep as the root ball or slightly deeper, and fill it with water. Gently break away the peat pot or loosen tangled roots.

the top rim and the bottom of the pot so the roots can escape easily. If the roots are tangled up or caked solid, use your finger to break them free.

Plant Spacing

How closely you space your new plants will depend on how large they will ultimately grow. Here are some examples.

- Smaller plants such as mustard, dill, and cilantro only spread about 6 inches wide.

- Teucrium, parsley, basil, summer savory, sage, and upright forms of thyme and sweet marjoram spread about 12 inches wide.

- French sorrel, chives, tarragon, and Greek oregano spread about 18 inches wide.

- Catnip, lovage, lavender, anise hyssop, and creeping thyme can spread to 2 feet wide.

- Angelica and mint can spread 3 feet or more across.

Fertilizer

In a well-prepared soil, a mulch of compost an inch thick is all the fertilizer that many herbs need. You may not have to fertilize herbs from the Mediterranean region at all because they develop the best fragrance and

How Many Plants Will You Need?

Determining just how much of any one herb to grow depends a lot on your tastes and how big each plant grows. A single mint plant can spread so quickly that it can keep you in mint tea, mint jelly, mint potpourri, and mint vinegar all summer. However, a single plant of dill will only produce a few tablespoons of seeds. If you like to use dill frequently, you'll need a dozen or more plants to produce the supply you need. Here are some potential yields of some common herbs.

Light Yields	Medium Yields	Abundant Yields
Anise (seeds and flowers)	Basil (foliage)	Catnip (foliage)
Caraway thyme (foliage)	Chervil (foliage)	Chives (foliage)
Chamomile (flowers)	Dill (foliage)	English thyme (foliage)
Chives (flowers)	French sorrel (foliage)	Lemon balm (foliage)
Coriander (seeds)	Rosemary (foliage)	Lovage (foliage)
Cumin (seeds)	Sage (foliage)	Mint (foliage)
Dill (seeds and foliage)	Summer savory (foliage)	Oregano (foliage)
Mustard (seeds)	Sweet marjoram (foliage)	Sweet Annie artemisia (foliage and flowers)
	Thyme (foliage)	Sweet woodruff (foliage and flowers)

Fertilization Schedule

Tailor your fertilization schedule according to (1) the kind of plant you grow, (2) whether or not the herb is a heavy feeder, and (3) the kind of soil you have. Barren, sandy soil will need more fertilizer than rich, loamy or clay soil. Fertilize herbs grown in pots of peat-moss–based growing mixes regularly because they have no reserve of nutrients. The following suggestions will help you time your fertilizer applications correctly.

- The most critical time to fertilize is when you are planting new herbs. A dose of water-soluble fertilizer at that time can help them start growing and rooting more rapidly.

- If you are growing seed crops, such as caraway, dill, and anise, give them another light fertilizer boost as they flower.

- Herbs you grow for their green foliage, such as arugula, can take fish-emulsion fertilizer every 3 weeks.

- Annual herbs such as basil that you harvest frequently will resprout more quickly if you give them a shot of balanced organic fertilizer after each harvest.

- For fruiting crops such as chile peppers, provide a higher nitrogen fertilizer until midsummer and then switch to a blend higher in phosphorus and potassium.

Divide perennial herbs such as chives by digging up a clump and separating it with gardening forks into two or more small clumps.

© Kevin Kennefick

Herbs That Don't Tolerate Division

A few herbs are best to leave growing undivided. They include annual and biennial herbs, monkshood, sweet bay, burdock, and fennel. Angelica and lovage are questionable.

the mature bulbs and snap off the new bulbs that grow around or in it. You may end up with up to a dozen or more new plants each year. Be careful that you don't cut the bulbs when you dig them up; this makes them susceptible to rotting. And be sure to label the bulbs and keep them in a cool, airy location if you don't replant them immediately.

Some plants that spread with vigor — such as mints, bee balm, and quickly creeping kinds of thyme — may need dividing every one or two years, depending on how compact you need to keep them. Others such as tarragon and upright forms of thyme need dividing every three years to keep them from getting too woody and unproductive.

The Dirt on Underground Growth

Perennial herbs that are naturally on the move — the ones that send runners across the soil — are a snap to divide with a little bit of careful shoveling. Those that form a dense clump require more care to unearth successfully, divide, and return — mostly intact — to the soil. Here are some examples of what you'll encounter:

Bulbs, Cloves, and Corms:

Perennial onions, garlic, saffron.

Creeping Herbs:

Thyme, oregano, bee balm, mint, English pennyroyal, sweet woodruff, artemisias, yarrow, oregano, lamb's ears, Roman chamomile.

Clump-Forming Herbs That Can Be Divided:

Lady's mantle, lemon balm, catnip, chives, French sorrel, winter savory, hyssop, rue, sage, tarragon, germander, catmint.

Divide creeping or clump-forming herbs as soon as the shoots begin to appear in spring or as the foliage starts dying back in fall. Choose spring if the herb blooms in summer or fall or is less than reliably hardy. Choose fall for spring bloomers or reliably hardy herbs you didn't get around to dividing in spring. (See p. 129 for dividing plants in the fall.)

To divide, dig as deeply as possible around all four sides of a plant and pull up the root ball surrounded with plenty of earth. Keep the root ball moist and out of direct sun. Use a shovel, knife, or axe to split off healthy young sections to propagate. How large the new sections will be is up to you, as long as each has at least one shoot and root. If you divide a big herb into a few medium-sized pieces, they will still look full. If you make one plant into many small ones, they may take some time to gain reasonable size. Replant the larger divisions right away. Start very small divisions in pots until they get big enough to survive in the garden.

Runners Make New Plants

Mints, bee balm, and oregano send creeping stems across the soil, which give you a handy source of new plants at your fingertips. If you lift one runner, you'll find it sprouts roots regularly along its length. Simply slice off one or more rooted section and replant in fresh moist soil or in a pot. You'll soon have a flourishing young plant.

By late spring, you have a good beginning on your herb garden. Perennials from previous years have grown large enough to propagate from; many herbs are ready for first harvest. It is time to face those weeds before they gain control of the garden.

CONTROLLING WEEDS

*D*eal with weeds as they arise and you can prevent problems with them in future weeks and years. The warmth of late spring encourages weed seeds to sprout; now is also a good time to pull out perennial weeds such as dock, dandelion, and morning glory and stray lawn grass that you missed the previous year. Take advantage of this time to get rid of weed seedlings and perennial weeds before they take over your herbs!

Unearth perennial weeds when the soil is moist. Grasp them near the base and pull out the roots. Or use a hoe to help loosen the roots before you pull. Try to get out all the roots; track down and pull out any left behind when you pulled out the plant.

Hoe or pull annual weeds such as chickweed, pigweed, lamb's quarters, and crabgrass as they arise. Be sure to get them before they go to seed and sprinkle hundreds of weed seeds around the garden. I hoe up the newly arisen weeds in my herb garden at least once a week. And then I pull up the big weeds, concentrating on areas where they come up through creeping herbs. I also pull weeds by hand if they arise at the perimeter of smaller herbs, where they're harder to see and impossible to get at with a hoe. If the weed is large and close to a small herb, I'll cut it off or hold the soil down around the base of the herb so it won't come up with the weed.

If you weed on a regular schedule, you will see the number of new weeds begin to diminish. When you've got the weeds under control, you can mulch to prevent more weeds from sprouting. Use a 2- to 4-inch layer of wood chips, shredded bark, or compost for an attractive ornamental mulch. Straw and unsprayed, weed-free grass clippings make a more utilitarian mulch.

LAYERING

$\mathcal{A}$nother way to propagate herbs is by layering them — letting long shoots develop roots while they are still attached to the parent plant. Layered shoots grow more vigorously than severed cuttings and have enough energy to produce roots in profusion. This is a good project for late spring.

Find a flexible lower stem on herbs such as santolina, winter savory, sage, tarragon, thyme, and rosemary. Bend it down to the ground and make a small nick in the bark where you want roots to grow. You may need to pin the stem to the ground with a peg or stick. Then cover it with soil. Keep the area moist but not wet, and the layered plant should root over a period of weeks or months. When a sturdy set of roots develops, cut the layered shoot free from the parent plant just beyond the roots. Replant into a prepared garden bed or put it in a pot to mature a bit longer before transplanting. Rosemary layers very well, so it is a good herb to use for your first attempt at layering.

© Kevin Kennefiek

You can obtain a new rosemary plant by a technique known as "layering." Bend a flexible stem down to the ground and make a small nick in the bark where you want roots to grow. Gently secure it to the ground with wire or soil before you cover it. Keep it moist and the layered shoot will root quickly. After roots develop, cut the shoot from the parent plant just beyond the roots.

CHAPTER 7

SUMMER IN THE HERB GARDEN

By summer, the garden has filled out. Mints are creeping on their stolons; lemon balm has risen to knee-high; angelica towers 5 feet tall. Summer becomes a bonanza for the gardener.

This season is ideal for herbs of Mediterranean origin — they thrive in sun and heat. The quick-growing, cool season plants — such as cilantro and mustard — that so bravely dealt with spring chills now go to seed, then melt away. Biennial or perennial herbs that prefer cool weather — plants such as parsley, lovage, and angelica — will pass the summer peacefully if you keep the soil cool and moist around them. You can help them out in hot climates by providing them with some shade in the hottest part of the afternoon.

In the warmth of the day, the aromas of the herbs will surround you as you walk or work among them. Most essential oils responsible for this aroma will peak as your herbs prepare to flower — bringing your activities to a critical point. Cut herbs quickly and preserve their rich flavor for the winter ahead. As summer ripens, your herbs will follow along with it.

In summer, mint may emerge in the thyme; catnip seedlings might appear snuggled up to the lovage; chive seedlings can elbow their way through a mat of yarrow. Keep a close eye out for the plants that become too aggressive. When herbs cross the line — stepping beyond "vigorous" into "weedy" — they are ripe for division and harvest. Dig up whole sections of them to use or move elsewhere in the garden.

While some herbs are spreading, you may find others are struggling with weeds, pests, or diseases. You may need to use some troubleshooting and problem-preventing tactics. You also might want to start more of your favorite herbs now to enjoy during fall and winter. This chapter will tell you how to do all of these things.

(Opposite page)

Blossoming santolina and lavender mark the beginning of summer in the herb garden.

Photo: © Karen Bussolini / Positive Images

101

And finally, when you have baskets full of fresh, aromatic herbs, you'll need plenty of ideas for how to use them. When days become too hot to be comfortable outdoors, retreat to a cool spot and try an herb project or two. (See Part Four.) Learn how to dry and freeze herbs; make pesto, herb sugars, and wreaths.

HARVESTING PERENNIALS & ANNUALS

*H*arvesting can be an art, or you can keep it a casual pleasure — take your choice. It's always all right to pluck herbs as you need them, which is the casual approach. No matter when you pick them, garden-fresh herbs beat commercially processed herbs hands down.

If you want to harvest a quantity of herbs for freezing or drying, capture them in bud, when the essential oil content is extra high. If you pick flowers to dry and use in wreaths, you need to capture them before the buds fully open.

© Kevin Kennefick

Spreading herbs such as thyme will look more natural and less "shorn" after harvest if you gather a bundle in your hand and cut it off with lawn clippers.

Harvesting Hints

Here are some harvesting tips from top herb enthusiasts. Author Madelene Hill recommends you start harvesting when you put the plant in the ground. Nip a little off the top right away and keep harvesting like that all through the growing season to get tender, rich-flavored leaves. If you wait to do all your harvesting in the middle of summer, you may only get sparse woody stems without much good foliage.

Nurseryman Tom DeBaggio says herbs such as thyme with upright or semi-upright growth habits can become woody as they age, which increases the chance of winter injury and restricts foliage growth. To avoid this, prune at an early stage and trim most of the new growth regularly through the growing season.

With herbs such as oregano, DeBaggio says the best time to harvest is when flower buds appear — about 60 days after growth begins in spring. Prune to within 6 inches of the ground, leaving some leaves. If the plant has become woody, prune the plant back to half or three-quarters of its new growth. You may be able to harvest again, but not after 45 days from the first expected hard freeze.

Culinary Harvests at a Glance

Seeds	Leaves	Edible Flowers	Roots
Anise	Anise hyssop	Anise	Angelica
Caraway	Chervil	Basil	Caraway
Celery	Cilantro	Bee balm	Fennel
Coriander	Dill	Borage	Ginger
Cumin	Fennel	Calendula	Hamburg parsley
Dill	French sorrel	Chamomile	Horseradish
Fennel	Lemon balm	Chives	Lovage
Fenugreek	Lemon verbena	Dill	
Lovage	Lovage	Garlic chives	
Mustard	Mustard	Lavender	
Nasturtium	Nasturtium	Mint	
	Oregano	Nasturtium	
	Perilla		
	Rosemary		
	Sage		
	Salad burnet		
	Savory		
	Sweet marjoram		
	Tarragon		
	Thyme		

If Your Timing Is Off

If you miss the prime harvest season for your favorite herb — perhaps while you are away on vacation — you may not notice a big change in the quality of herbs such as tarragon and thyme. Keep on snipping sprigs through the growing season. But others, once they begin to set seed, focus so much energy on seed development that little energy is left for the foliage. Just watch mustard foliage dwindle away to almost nothing and the upper leaves of flowering lovage yellow and fade as the plants produce seed. If you're not ready to give up on these herbs, give the plant immediate attention. You'll probably still be able to find some leaves worth using.

Other herbs, such as basil and arugula, may undergo flavor changes. Arugula, when exposed to heat, will develop stronger flavor. Basil, when exposed to cool weather, can taste slightly metallic. If you don't like what you taste, make a note to harvest them earlier next year.

But even if you find your herbs have passed their prime, you might still find something else to harvest from them.

- Instead of foliage, harvest the flavorful seeds of herbs such as mustard and lovage.

- Harvest and dry flower heads of thyme, basil, and oregano for color and fragrance in wreaths and bouquets.

- Let the seed of salad burnet, holy basil, and calendula self-sow and provide plants for next year.

For good harvest timing, get to know when your herbs are likely to flower. Unless you are forewarned or you inspect each plant every day, the critical bud stage could slip by before you realize it. (See Chapter 5 for blooming sequences by season.)

If you need a large quantity of herb sprigs for freezing or drying, you can cut the stems of most leafy herbs back by one-third to two-thirds of their length. Many annual herbs and some vigorously growing perennial herbs will resprout for additional harvests. Harvest young perennials lightly — if at all — during their first year to help them get established. Stop cutting perennial herbs in cold climates by early fall to maintain winter hardiness.

The best time to cut is in the morning after the dew dries and before the heat of mid-day. The evening is also a good time for harvesting herbs and a great way for you to relax at the end of the day. And according to one university study, basil picked in the evening stored longer than basil cut in the morning.

If you want to dry herbs, harvest them after a couple of rain-free days. The leaves and stems will be less succulent and easier to dry.

Choose your harvesting technique based on the type of plant and whether you wish to use leaves, seeds, roots, or flowers.

(Top Left) Pinch back the the top growth of basils so that the plants will continue to provide you with tender leaves to harvest throughout the summer.

(Bottom Left) To harvest chives, cut the plant back to the ground. You may get a second harvest in the same season.

(Top Right) To harvest parsley, remove the larger, outer leaves at the base of the plant. The center of the plant will continue to put out new growth.

Quick Tricks with Herbs

Sometimes in summer it seems that everything happens at once. When half a dozen herbs are prime for harvesting, you may also be planning a dinner party or getting ready to take a vacation. When your hands are full but the garden needs you, you can stay calm and cool if you're organized. The following tips can help keep everything under control.

Establish some priorities. Pick the herbs that will lose quality if you don't get to them today, catching mustard greens, arugula, and basil before

Harvesting

Method	Suitable Herbs	Technique	Comments
Pinch or shear	Basil, sweet marjoram, perilla, oregano, sage, rosemary, thyme	Pinch or shear 2–3 inches of shoot tips, or tender young leaves.	Encourages bushy growth.
Pick individual leaves	Parsley, lovage, chervil, coriander, mustard, French sorrel, nasturtium	Cut off outer leaves at the base.	Inner leaves will continue to grow for your next harvest.
Pick individual leaves as soon as they reach full size	Dill, lemon verbena, salad burnet, basil, arugula, cilantro, French sorrel	Cut off leaves or flower buds as soon as they reach full size.	Remove flower buds of dill and salad burnet to extend the period of prime foliage harvest.
Cut down to the ground	Chives, garlic, or other Onion Family members	To harvest greens, cut the leaves close to the ground.	If you only cut them back part way, the base of the leaf will turn brown. With chives, you can cut back small clumps of leaves or the entire plant.
Gather seeds	Dill, coriander, anise, cumin, caraway	Wait until seed pods swell and begin to change color. Gather when they start to turn brown.	Finish drying seeds indoors (see Chapter 11 on drying herbs).
Dig roots	Horseradish, angelica, lovage, Hamburg parsley (and other herbs with aromatic roots)	Dig up roots when the plant begins to die back.	Unearth entire clumps of horseradish roots and replant small divisions or root cuttings. Dig and preserve entire Hamburg parsley root (it won't grow again from cuttings).
Collect flowers	Nasturtiums, chives, calendula, dill, borage, anise hyssop, lovage, thyme, basil, bee balm, mint, rosemary	Pick soon after the flowers open.	Serve them whole, or sprinkle the petals on salads or desserts. Use herb flowers to flavor herbal vinegar (see Chapter 11).

they flower. You could also pick the herbs that you enjoy the most or concentrate on the herbs that are the easiest to handle so you'll have more time for your other activities.

If you have a lot of herbs to dry in a dehydrator, harvest only one kind of herb at a time. This lets you fill up the dehydrator without worrying about mistaking identities. (Identifying herbs after they're dried can be difficult.)

If you've harvested a little more of a fresh herb than you can use today, put the sprigs in a glass of water on your kitchen counter to use tomorrow. Or put the glass in the refrigerator to keep sprigs fresh for a few days. Some herbs such as parsley, lovage, thyme, and rosemary will also last a few days in the refrigerator in a sealed plastic bag. But don't refrigerate basil — the cold temperatures can damage it.

If you are short on time and you need to preserve herbs quickly, toss them whole into a freezer bag and freeze them. Or drop them into a jar of vinegar.

Washing Herbs

If you haven't treated your herbs with pesticides, liquid fertilizers, or anything else unpleasant, they may not need much washing. You can rinse them off in the garden the night before you pick them. The plant will be fresh, clean, and dry by the following morning, and will only need light rinsing. But herbs that creep, grow under or along the ground, or have crinkled leaves (where soil can get lodged) or pest problems need thorough washing after harvest. Plants such as low-growing thyme and oregano can often be covered with soil. Herbs with puckered leaves such as lettuce-leaf basil can hide insects and grit in their folds and crevices. And herbs prone to insect infestation could be housing insects or their eggs. Wash them thoroughly.

Swish herbs around in a tub of cold water or hold them under gently running cold water so that you do not end up with an unexpected crunch in your lunch. And be especially careful to wash insects out of flower blossoms. If you spot any bugs inside, wash as described above, then dip the flowers in some vinegar water — one tablespoon of vinegar per cup of water — which helps eject insects fast.

SUMMER PLANTING

You can keep sowing herb seed in the summer to fill any vacant spaces in your garden with quick-growing, warm-season annuals such as basil, dill, summer savory, and sweet marjoram. In mid- to late summer, start cool-season cilantro, arugula, and mustard for a fall harvest. If your summers are very hot or dry, you can wait until fall to replant, or start the seeds indoors and keep them well watered, mulched, and lightly shaded when you transplant them outdoors.

Slip in those pots of herbs you've been meaning to plant but haven't gotten around to until now. Or start biennial plants growing where the spring crops left off. They'll be ready to flower next year if you plant them now.

© Paula Craft

Many herbs benefit from a bit of shade in the hottest part of summer; here, sage, lemon balm, and thyme.

For summer planting, purchase herbs grown in containers because they have a fairly large, undisturbed root system. But some container-grown plants may be rootbound by now. You'll have to loosen or cut off the interwoven outer roots before planting. You can also move an herb or transplant a large division during mild summer weather (but not hot or dry weather) as long as you dig up most of the roots and leave them securely packed in soil. But bareroot plants, small seedlings, or tiny divisions can suffer if you try to plant them when nature turns the heat up and the rain off.

Just as in spring, you'll have to prepare the soil well before you plant new herbs. It's especially important to get rid of weeds that popped up in the summer warmth and to amend soil that may have become depleted from growing an earlier crop. Here's a summer soil preparation and planting checklist to refer to when you're ready to put in more herbs.

- Pull perennial weeds out, roots and all. Hoe to uproot annual weeds.

- Make sure the soil is loose and light, not compacted and bricklike. If it's compacted, loosen it with a spade and hoe or a rototiller.

- If you're recycling the area after a spring or winter planting, replenish the organic matter by adding an inch or more of compost.

- If the area has not been draining well, improve the drainage now. Dig down deep to break up any compacted subsurface soil layers. You can also raise the bed, elevating it several inches so rain and irrigation water will drain out. It also helps to add organic matter to loosen up the soil and allow water to move through the soil freely.

Even herbs that are drought-tolerant need water until they develop a substantial root system to tolerate dry soil. Run a soaker hose around the planting site and let it saturate the soil deeply once or twice a week. Mulch around the new plants with a several-inch layer of untreated grass clippings, straw, or shredded bark. Or poke a small hole in the bottom of a plastic jug. Sink it into the soil near the young herb and fill it with water. The water will trickle slowly out, providing a long-lasting source of moisture.

To keep herbs from wilting in summer heat — especially the younger, more tender herbs — plant them in a place that gets afternoon shade. You can place them to the east of taller plants or walls. Or set up a temporary sunblock using a piece of wood, an old license plate, a shovel stuck in the ground, or any other upright object.

SUMMER WATERING IDEAS

*Q*uick-growing annual herbs such as basil, moisture-loving perennials such as angelica and sweet woodruff, cut-and-come-again herbs, and new seedlings or transplants grow best if you can keep the soil evenly moist. Usually an inch of water a week is okay, but herbs need more water in hot, dry months and sandy soils and less in cool, wet months and mulched or clay soils. Many Mediterranean herbs can get by on less moisture; they favor arid parts of the country or people with wells that cannot support too much garden watering. During our last severe summer drought, I watched my lawn turn totally brown while my thyme and savory marched along beautifully green.

It might be tempting to pull out the hose and sprinkle the herbs by hand. I know I've done that occasionally. But even after standing there sprinkling for 5 minutes, I found that not even the top half-inch of soil was moist. (A lot of the water had hit the ground and run off.) I hadn't succeeded in getting any moisture down to the roots where the plants could use it. I had good intentions but wasn't getting the job done.

To water more effectively, you'll need to use some kind of sprinkler, soaker hose, or other form of irrigation. Our old standard, the overhead sprinker, has proven to be the most inefficient. It's annoying to move it around the garden if you crush plants beneath the snaking hose. And then, when you turn it on, it waters weeds, walks, a bit of the lawn, and — oh yes — some herbs too. A large percentage evaporates back into the air on a sunny day. Some of the droplets pound the ground and roll off; they have more size and velocity than the earth can absorb. Only a small part of all that water reaches your herbs.

It is more challenging, but a more economical way to water is with drip irrigation or soaker hoses. Both systems release water at soil level — directly to the cultivated plants — not to the air, weeds, and other vegetation. They let water trickle out gently, over time soaking the soil deeply without compressing it. And they won't wet plant foliage, so they reduce the occurrence of fungus diseases.

At the most basic (and inexpensive) level, you can water short rows of herbs with soaker hoses. Hook them up to the

Monitoring Rainfall

*K*eep track of the amount of rain that's fallen so you'll have a good idea of when you need to provide extra water. It can be hard to gauge just how much a day-long drizzle supplies and even harder to eyeball the net gain from a drenching downpour. So spend a few dollars and buy a rain gauge, a clear plastic rain collector with a gauge on the side that indicates how many inches have fallen. Or leave a margarine tub in an open area of the garden. Measure the depth of the water with a ruler after every rain. If at the end of the week, nature has come up short on water, you can supply it.

faucet and they'll ooze droplets of water along their length. But they tend to put out far more water at the top of the hose and far less at the bottom, plus they easily become kinked or clogged.

If you can afford to spend a little extra, you can buy drip irrigation lines that are regulated to provide an even amount of water from each emitter hole. That way, every herb will get its fair share. You can go a step further and buy whole irrigation systems, networks of tubing and connecting lines that can cover the entire garden. The ideal spacing of the emitters and lines and the volume of water they need to pump out will vary with the kinds of plants you're growing and the kind of soil you have. So ask for professional advice before settling on a system. If you are handy around the house, you can install most drip systems yourself. Be certain the lines will wet the soil around the entire plant, instead of being content with moistening only one side. But if you're boggled by the jumble of tubes, emitters, connecters, and more, it might be worth paying for professional installation to get the job done right.

If you want to install your own irrigation system, first sketch out the area that needs watering. Decide whether you want to run the irrigation lines along rows, as in a cutting garden, or around groups of plants, as in a landscape bed. Do you want to water with a drip emitter, good for individual plants, or a low-volume sprinkler? The sprinkler can water low herbs in a variety of different spray patterns so the water soaks the planted area, and not paths or open areas. Sketch in what you need, find the right pieces to order, then assemble and start up the system as directed.

A rain gauge monitors rainfall. Soaker hoses efficiently carry water directly to the plants' roots.

TROUBLESHOOTING IN THE HERB GARDEN

If you plant herbs that can thrive in your climate and give them the right balance of sun and soil, you'll have fewer problems with pests and diseases. The aromas of herbs repel *many* pests, but because aromatic repellents don't work on *all* pests, you'll still need to keep an eye out for occasional problems.

Troubleshooting Insect Pests

Insect Pest	Plants Affected	Symptoms	Control
Tarnished Plant Bug 	Cilantro, anise hyssop, nasturtium	Shoots curl; new growth dies; plants wilt.	Cover susceptible herbs with floating row covers or spray with insecticidal soap. Clean up old garden debris well in fall to remove hibernating bugs.
Slugs/Snails 	French sorrel, basil, sage, or any plant with soft growth	Large holes leave ragged openings on leaves.	Eliminate rocks, logs, thick mulch, or other debris. Improve garden drainage. Trap slugs in saucers of beer. Change the traps regularly. Surround plants with wood ashes, cinders, or sharp sand, which are uncomfortable for soft-bodied pests.
Aphids 	Rose, oregano, nasturtium, angelica, bee balm, basil, calendula	Sticky droppings feed black, sooty molds.	Wash aphids off with a strong blast from the garden hose, or spray with insecticidal soap.
Whiteflies 	Scented geranium, basil, tarragon, lemon verbena	Small whiteflies dart around when you brush the plant foliage.	You can catch whiteflies on sticky yellow traps or spray the plants with insecticidal soap.
Spider Mites	Mint, lemon verbena, nasturtium, oregano, basil, miniature rose, rosemary, sage, thyme	Plant is covered with fine webs; leaf surface appears speckled or dull.	Use a strong spray with the hose or spray with insecticidal soap or pyrethrum.

Troubleshooting Diseases

Disease	Plants Affected	Symptoms	Control
Virus Diseases 	Mints and other herbs	Leaves suddenly become colored with yellow streaks or spots and grow strangely curled.	No cure, but control sucking insects such as aphids or leaf hoppers that spread them. Blast disease spreaders off the plant with a hose or spray them with insecticidal soap. Dig up and throw away (don't compost) infected plants so they won't infect other plants.
Stem, Root, and Crown Rot 	Lamb's ears, thyme, Greek oregano, tender lavenders, sage, gray and green santolina, winter savory, germander, catmints, angelica, rue, garlic, or any other herb grown in soggy soil	Rotting tissue turns black and slimy. When lower parts of the plant die, the rest of the plant will die. Rot can be caused by a variety of diseases and once they're started, it's impossible to save the infected portions.	Dig up and throw away (but don't compost) diseased parts of the plant. Replant healthy sections in a different part of the garden. Raise the original bed or install a better drainage system before you replant.
Powdery Mildew 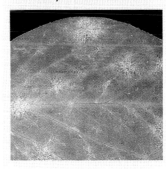	Yarrow, bee balm, roses, lemon balm, rosemary, and others	Leaves are coated with gray fuzz.	For prevention, give plants plenty of space for air circulation. Cut affected bee balm foliage back to the ground and it should resprout clean. Note: Look for mildew-resistant varieties.

All photos © Ron West, with the exception of the Stem Rot photo © Renée Lax

You're more likely to see pests or diseases if a plant is struggling with too much or too little sun, water, or nutrients. Then it's weaker and easier for pests and diseases to attack. Plenty of sun and free-moving air also help discourage problems because they keep herb foliage dry so that disease spores can't germinate there.

If problems are particularly severe on one kind of herb, perhaps you don't have the right situation for it. Try growing something else there. Rosemary and sage are particularly prone to root rot in rich, clay soil, especially in humid climates. But most mints will thrive under those same conditions.

Identifying Problems

Here are some common pests and diseases you might find on your herbs, with identification and control suggestions (see chart on p. 112).

Tarnished Plant Bug. These are small (¼-inch long) brownish bugs, with black-rimmed, yellowish triangles on their upper wings. They'll eat just about anything, and can even spread bacterial diseases to some of your herbs and also to any Cabbage Family members you grow.

Slugs/Snails. These slimy, creeping pests hide in moist places under mulch or rocks and climb up plants to riddle the leaves or tender growth.

Aphids. These are small, soft-bodied pests that cling to new growth or the undersides of leaves, sometimes in large numbers. They suck plant sap and often leave behind sticky droppings that feed black, sooty molds.

Whiteflies. When you keep herbs indoors during winter, they may be attacked by whiteflies — small, white, flying insects that dart around when you brush the plant foliage. You can catch whiteflies on sticky yellow traps or spray the plants with insecticidal soap.

Spider Mites. Spider mites are so tiny that you may not see them until they cover your plant with fine webs. The eight-legged relatives of spiders thrive in hot and dry weather; they're perfectly happy indoors in the winter. They feed underneath the leaves, causing the leaf surface to look speckled or dull; and they leave tiny webs strung from leaf to leaf.

How You Can Prevent or Control Problems

For herbs to remain safe to eat and use, shy away from toxic chemical agents when problems strike. Fortunately, there are safe and effective techniques and products that you can use to deal with problems without worry. Here are some of the most effective procedures.

Provide Good Air Circulation. When planting, give herbs enough room to grow without crowding. And in spring, thin out overgrown and crowded plants so air can circulate freely around them. This reduces the incidence of many fungus diseases such as mildew, leaf spot, and stem rot.

Provide Well-Drained Soil. Most herbs need soil that will drain freely to avoid root, crown, and stem rot. If your soil is not well drained, learn how to recognize and deal with poorly drained soil (see Chapter 4).

Plant Resistant Cultivars. If herbs are regularly troubled by diseases, look for disease-resistant cultivars. Although these are not common among traditional culinary herbs, you can find disease resistance in a few of the more ornamental herbs. 'Gardenview Scarlet' is an example of a bee balm cultivar resistant to powdery mildew; the Meidiland shrub roses are resistant or tolerant to serveral diseases.

Go Light on Fertilizer. Most herbs need moderate to light fertilizing. If you feed them too much nitrogen, they'll grow soft and lush, becoming an easy target for slugs, snails, rot, and other diseases. For more information on fertilizing, see p. 92–94.

Interplant. If you have an herb that pests routinely visit, try planting it amid other kinds of herbs or even in a flower bed. Mingling it with plants of different fragrances makes it harder for pests to find.

Thinning Bee Balm to Prevent Disease

Bee balm tends to be susceptible to powdery mildew disease, which can destroy its good looks and culinary usefulness within weeks. But you can help prevent the attack of powdery mildew by thinning out every third stem in early summer, when the stems are 1 to 2 inches tall. This will allow more air to circulate through the plant and make it harder for mildew to get started.

Rotate Plants. Move related plants to new locations every year or planting cycle as a problem-solving technique. It helps keep pests and diseases from building up. Herbs are not as prone to pest problems as many flowers and vegetables, but problems do occasionally occur, and this is a healthy way to deal with them.

With annual and biennials, change the planting sites for Carrot Family members such as parsley, caraway, dill, Florence fennel; Mint Family members such as basil, summer savory, sweet marjoram; and Mustard Family members such as arugula and mustard.

Rotate perennial herbs, too, if they suffer disease problems. For instance, if you remove a rose infested with black spot, don't plant another rose in that spot. Instead replant something like tarragon or lovage that is not susceptible to the disease spores that are sure to be there.

Attract Beneficial Insects. Many members of the insect kingdom — such as lady beetles, parasitic wasps, lacewings, hoverflies, and soldier beetles, will eat or parasitize pests living in your garden. You can attract beneficial insects by keeping a variety of flowers blooming all during the growing season; flowers provide pollen and nectar, an alternative food source. Beneficial insects especially enjoy the nectar and pollen of herbs in the Mint Family (mints, thyme, savory, and rosemary) and the umbrella-shaped heads of flowers of plants in the Carrot Family (dill, fennel, and angelica). These plants help attract parasitic wasps, lady beetles, lacewings, hoverflies, tachinid flies, and other garden good guys who will patrol your garden with zeal as long as you don't kill them off with pesticides and you provide a little water or shelter among the plants.

When you have done all you could, but you still have some pests and/or disease in your herb garden, try the following suggestions.

Insecticial Soaps. The salts contained in insecticidal soaps kill soft-bodied insects such as aphids, caterpillars, flies, lacebugs, leafhoppers, mealybugs, mites, scales, spittlebugs, thrips, and whiteflies. They have little effect on most beneficial insects and pollinators.

© Rosalind Creasy

Dill and parsley are among the herbs that attract beneficial insects to the garden.

Refined Oil Sprays. These are lightweight versions of the old dormant oil sprays that you can apply to plants during the growing season. They coat and kill pests such as aphids, caterpillars, leafminers, mealybugs, mites, scales, and whiteflies.

Baking Soda Spray. You might want to experiment with this nontoxic spray for blackspot and mildew — although it has not yet been confirmed that it is useful for herbs. Combine 1 tablespoon baking soda, 1 tablespoon vegetable oil, a drop of liquid dishwashing soap, and 1 gallon water. Mix well and spray every 5 to 7 days during humid weather or when you see the first sign of either disease.

Botanical Sprays of Hot Peppers, Garlic, and Herb Oils. When you combine the aromatic qualities of many different herbs, you can come up with a powerful natural pest repellent. (But use it cautiously at first because the strength will vary and the formulation could affect different herbs in different ways.) Try blending 2 hot peppers, a few cloves of garlic, and some citrus peels or lemon-scented thyme together in a blender. Add 2 tablespoons of this concentrate and a little dishwashing soap to 1 quart of water and use as a spray.

WORKING OUT THE WEEDS

*H*ang in there with your weeding and mulching to keep out any late-arriving weeds. Keep the garden clear this year, and you'll have an even smaller problem next year. Be sure to snag annual weeds that bolt to seed when you're not looking during the heat of summer. Work loose perennial weeds before they grow entangled with your herbs.

Be especially wary of look-alike weeds that grow in and beside your herbs. When young, weed foliage can look similar to your herbs; the weeds can be easy to miss unless you look carefully under and beside herb plants. When you harvest herbs, do a last quality-control check for anything that looks even slightly out of place, so weeds won't end up in your food.

Here are a couple of common inedible lookalikes that you want to be sure to eliminate:

Buttercup. *Ranunculus acris* is a common, yellow-flowered weed of vacant fields that grows in the eastern and northwestern United States. Buttercups contain an irritating substance, ranunculin, which can blister your hands when you handle it or upset your stomach if you eat it fresh. But, fortunately, it's nontoxic when dried.

You'll know buttercup by its glossy, yellow, open-faced flowers that erupt into bloom in late spring. Its leaves are deeply lobed and its stems reach 3 feet high. It has 5 petals, ½-inch wide.

Bittersweet nightshade. *Solanum dulcamara* is a poisonous weed that grows in eastern and north-central parts of the United States. It grows into vines up to 15 feet long, with leaves that are lobed at the base. It has violet flowers with golden centers during summer, which ripen into glossy red berries that can attract children.

Indian tobacco. *Lobelia inflata* is a toxic annual common in open soil around eastern and central North America. It was once smoked by native Americans, but eating it can cause sickness, even death. Indian tobacco grows a foot or taller and has long, narrow and toothed, light green leaves, which unfortunately make excellent herb lookalikes when young. You can identify it from June to October by looking for the small, light blue or blue-violet, two-lipped flowers that appear near leaf bases or in clusters at the top of the plant.

Jimsonweed. *Datura stramonium* is a nasty customer present in farmlands in southern and northeastern states. It came into my garden in a load of topsoil I added a couple of years ago, and continues to emerge regularly. It's poisonous enough to kill a person. You can identify young plants by the toothed oval leaves, which can reach 8 inches long, and prickly green or purple stem. In late summer or fall, the plant produces handsome white or purple trumpet-shaped flowers, which develop into prickly fruits.

MULCH

To keep these and other weeds at bay, you need to continue to mulch. In summer, mulching will also insulate the soil, moderate temperature swings, and keep soil moist. (You might only need to water half as much when your garden is covered with a thick blanket of mulch!)

Applying Mulch in Summer

Material	Thickness
Bark Nuggets	4 to 6 inches
Bark Chips	3 to 4 inches
Coarsely Shredded Bark	2 inches
Finely Shredded Bark	1 inch
Straw	4 inches
Grass Clippings	1 to 2 inches
Shredded Leaves	2 inches
Coarse Sand	1 to 2 inches

But keep the mulch away from the base of your herbs so it won't encourage rotting. Use it cautiously on slug-infested, wet soil.

To maximize the advantages of summer mulch and limit the disadvantages, use mulches wisely. Apply fine-textured mulches in thinner layers so they won't suffocate the soil. Coarse-textured mulches, which won't retain as much moisture, can go on a little thicker. Here are some general guidelines to get you started.

- Use coarse sand underneath plants that need good drainage, to help prevent root and crown rot.

- Don't bother to use peat moss as a mulch. It's too fine-textured and lightweight to work well. And it dries into an umbrella-like layer that rainwater will roll off of instead of sinking into.

DEADHEADING & REJUVENATING

Once an herb is done flowering, the seeds mature. For most plants, especially annuals, producing seed becomes a high priority — one that consumes most of the plant's energy so it can't produce or sometimes even maintain the foliage it has. The leaves you'd hoped to harvest may discolor or drop off, which is neither attractive nor productive. Herbs such

© Kevin Kennefick

© Kevin Kennefick

© Kevin Kennefick

(Top Left) Deadheading calendula flowers encourages new flowers to form.

(Top Right) Deadhead herbs such as lady's mantle by pruning back spent flowers.

(Bottom Right) Cut back dead lavender seedpods to allow the plant to put out new growth.

as basil, dill, French sorrel, and lovage seem to shrink to nothing after flowering unless you remove the flowers of developing seed heads. (Some herbs become as bad as weeds if the seeds get loose in the garden.) To keep your herb foliage fresh and also encourage a second period of bloom for some herbs (e.g., catmint), remove the faded flowers on any herb except those you harvest for seed. This is called "deadheading."

You can deadhead in several ways. Use shears to remove upright pods that stand above the foliage on winter savory, bush basil, santolina, and lavender. You also can shear thyme, oregano, or lemon balm plants, cutting and using flowers and foliage. Use hand-held pruning shears to clip off the fading flowers just above a set of leaves on mint, dill (if you're growing it primarily for its foliage), basil, yarrow, lady's mantle, bee balm, and other herbs. To encourage reflowering on orna mental herbs such as yarrow, bee balm, catmint, lavender, nasturtiums, calendulas, violas, pinks, roses, and anise hyssop, cut the old flowers off just above young flower buds developing lower on the stem.

SUMMER DOWN TIME

*T*he heat is on; the humidity is high. You don't want to go outside except to race to your air-conditioned car or to jump in the cool pool. But you don't need to call it quits in the garden. Do what you need to care for your garden, then return indoors and dabble with herbs in an environment that's more congenial.

Revise your planting arrangement on paper. If your spring garden had a color combination that struck you as awkward, if a tall plant weaseled its way to the foreground of the garden and blocked your view, if a plant that needed better drainage fell into a damp spot, now is a good time to make plans to set things right. Sketch it all out now so you can move the plants around when the weather is more moderate.

Take pictures of your herb garden each week as a reminder of what went well and what you could improve. Consider keeping a garden journal each year. It is a good place to map out what you have done and what you would like to do in the future.

Clean out the herb cupboard. Go through your old jars of dried herbs and give them all the sniff test. If they don't have a strong, clean aroma, throw them out and make a note to dry some more.

Reorganize the freezer herbs. You can make it easy to find flat packets of herbs in the freezer if you develop a filing system. Find a box that your herb packets will fit in and make labeled dividers for each kind of herb, like in an index card file. Then file all the herbs you've frozen and make a note to freeze more of the ones you're short on.

Herbs That Produce Enough Seeds to Be Weedy

Some herbs produce hundreds of seeds, which might spring up all over your garden and make your real weeds pale by comparison. You can capitalize on this by collecting their seeds to give away. Or for prolific-seeding herbs such as caraway, coriander, dill, mustard, and fennel, gather all the seeds to use as flavorings. (Be sure to harvest newly ripened seed that hasn't had a chance to dry and fall to the ground. You also can put a catch cloth under the plants as you cut the seed heads.) With borage and chives, you can cut off all the newly opened flowers for salads. Deadhead regularly on other herbs, such as catnip, lemon balm, anise hyssop, sweet Annie artemisia, perilla, and French sorrel.

CHAPTER 8

FALL IN THE HERB GARDEN

As the growing season progresses, the days grow shorter and more limiting for plants, but the herb garden still remains active. Saffron crocuses lift their lavender heads; the golden stigmas, inside the flowers, contain fragrant spice. Pineapple sage is just beginning to flower and anise hyssop continues to bloom in profusion. Cool-season annuals such as calendula, arugula, and mustard are also coming on strong. They emerge from seed sown in summer to thrive in fall — even winter in mild climates. You also have plenty of parsley at this time of year; it stays green late into fall before dying back. If you mulch it thickly, it may even last long enough for you to use it for holiday feasts

Meanwhile, in cold climates, herbaceous perennials begin to grow more slowly; they start to transport vital nutrients to their underground roots so they can lay low when it gets cold. Woody herbs are hardening their new growth in preparation for weathering winter cold. It is time for you and your plants to prepare for winter. Bring in all the seeds, leaves, and roots that you will need. Harvest a bit extra for holiday gift-giving. Check for insects, especially whiteflies, before potting up herbs and bringing them indoors.

If you live in a warm climate with a long, mild winter, it could become one of your most productive seasons in the herb garden. When fall weather starts to get cool, you can grow cool-season annuals such as mustard, arugula, calendula, and onions. If your winters remain warm, however, you may find perennial herbs that need a dormancy period will begin to peter out. You could try to cut them back to stimulate dormancy and see if they will resprout fresh and renewed.

~

(Opposite page)

Parsley and sage seem to enjoy the cooler fall temperatures and may last into early winter even in cold areas.

~

In areas with cold autumn weather, dig up your warmth-loving annuals such as basil or 'Lemon Gem' marigolds and bring them indoors before they begin to grow limp and weary. These plants can give you pleasure deep into winter. Also move in tender perennials such as lemon verbena or rosemary that may not last the winter outdoors or that you can't live without during the cold months. For more details on growing herbs in containers, see Chapter 10.

When the first frost finally arrives and tender plants have turned black, it's time to clean up. Remove debris, tossing old stems, roots, and seed-free weeds on the compost pile. Cultivate vacant garden sites to make your garden look neat and to eliminate hiding places for pests and diseases.

Once the site is in good condition, you can get a head start on your planting. In colonial America, fall was one of the most popular times to plant hardy annual, biennial, and perennial herbs. In those days, storing seeds over the winter could be more precarious than sowing them and letting the seedlings fend for themselves. Fall planting still has many advantages today. You can get an extra early start and save yourself time in spring when you'll need it most. Fall is an opportune time to spend your energy preparing for a bountiful growing season the following year.

FALL HARVESTING

Up until this point, you've had the option of harvesting when the herbs were at their peak or taking a more leisurely approach and picking a few sprigs whenever you needed them. But now all bets are off. Early fall is your last chance to harvest most herbs before they go dormant for the winter. Think about the plant's natural growth patterns before you harvest. If an herb is an annual, it dies back completely in cold climates, so you should harvest annuals before they are killed by winter cold.

But if you harvest hardy woody perennials such as thyme, savory, and tarragon heavily now, you can weaken the plants. (It won't hurt to take a couple of sprigs, but discontinue heavy pruning of woody herbs and roses 45 days before you expect the first fall frost.) Also, don't harvest herbs that are susceptible to winterkill in your area unless you are cutting them back before bringing them indoors. Avoid heavy fall pruning on roses, evergreens, and other trees and shrubs that haven't yet fallen dormant. As long as woody plants are still growing, they could resprout with soft new twigs that are certain to be lost to winter cold.

Bringing Herbs Indoors

Bring in existing plants or make new ones by dividing them. About a month before the first fall frost, dig up the plants you want to keep indoors. Capture as many of the roots as you can. Mature plants, such as sweet marjoram, lavender, and scented geraniums, should be cut back by about one-third their full height to make them more manageable. (You can cut them back even more drastically if the root ball is small.) Put each one into a pot that's slightly bigger than its roots. Fill in the vacant area with a soilless growing mix. Let the plants get settled in the pots in a lightly shaded outdoor location for a week or so. Then move them into deeper shade for another week to get them ready to come indoors. Before frost arrives, bring tender herbs indoors to the window or light garden you've prepared.

When you pot up an herb, choose a pot that is slightly bigger than its rootball.

When Can You Expect Fall?

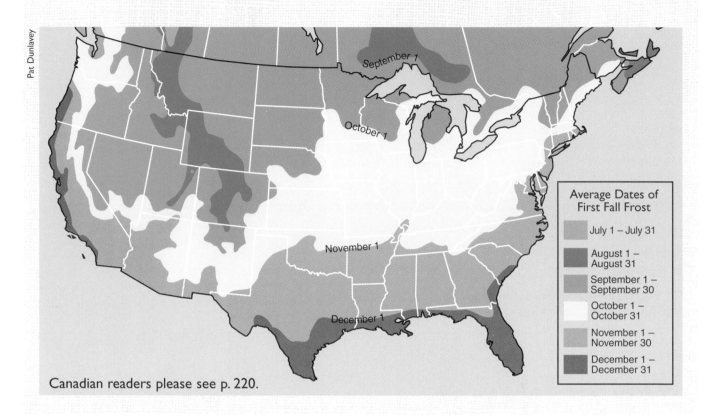

September 1

October 1

November 1

December 1

Average Dates of First Fall Frost

- July 1 – July 31
- August 1 – August 31
- September 1 – September 30
- October 1 – October 31
- November 1 – November 30
- December 1 – December 31

Canadian readers please see p. 220.

Pat Dunlavey

But let chives and garlic chives stay out through a month or so of winter cold before you bring them indoors; they will grow much better indoors if they get a short winter to trick them into thinking it's spring.

If conditions are right, they'll resprout and provide you with some fragrant foliage to harvest in midwinter.

Don't be surprised if your lemon verbena drops all its leaves due to the move indoors. This doesn't mean it's dead; it may only be dormant, which will save you from having to protect the leaves from spider mites. Keep it cool and dry until it resprouts, then you can begin to water and fertilize it again.

When your herbs are grouped together indoors, they may be more susceptible to pest problems. If you find whiteflies fluttering around the indoor herb garden, spray with insecticidal soap to kill mature flies and repeat until you get rid of newly hatched generations. Red spider mites may attack because the humidity is low. If so, use a pebble tray and fight them with insecticidal soap. (Pebbles allow you to rest herb plants over — not in — a tray of water.) To discourage diseases, remove dark, dead, and sickly growth, and scrub your pruning shears or knife in a solution of 1 part bleach to 10 parts water between each cut.

Fall Seeding

Work fresh seed into well-prepared soil in early fall. The plants may germinate now and spend winter as small seedlings, or they may germinate early in spring. For many perennials, such as those listed at the right for fall seeding, exposure to winter's alternating periods of warm and cool temperatures, freezing and thawing, and wet and dry soil can coax reluctant seeds out of their shells faster than spring sowing.

In warm climates, fall and winter are ideal times to plant cool-season herbs such as mustard, cilantro, calendula, and arugula. Sow the seed while the temperatures hover around 70°F or when cooler but mild weather can be expected to follow.

Herbs for Fall Seeding

Angelica	Mustard
Arugula	Parsley
Caraway	Pyrethrum
Dill	Soapwort
Garlic	Sweet cicely
Ginseng	Winter onions

BULB PLANTING

Fall is a great time for planting many bulbs, including landscape favorites such as daffodils and tulips (which you can dry to use in potpourri), but you also can grow herb bulbs such as garlic, saffron, and, in southern climates, short-day onions.

- Plant saffron, an autumn-blooming crocus, in late summer or early fall. Put the little corms in large groups so they'll stand out when they flower.

- Plant garlic cloves in September or October, about 6 weeks before the first fall frost. Set them about 1 inch deep and 4 inches apart in rich, well-drained soil. You'll harvest them in late summer or early fall of the following year.

- Plant short-day onions such as 'Granex' and 'Texas Supersweets' in climates with mild winter weather. Plant the seeds or seedlings when temperatures become cooler in fall, and harvest when the bulbs grow large and the foliage yellows.

Plant garlic cloves about 1 inch deep and 4 inches apart in rich, well-drained soil.

© Kevin Kennefick

EXTENDING THE SEASON

*I*f you want to keep your herbs growing longer into fall, you can protect them from frost. Surround upright herbs with 4 hay bales or a tomato cage. Cover open areas with clear or milky plastic to make a mini-greenhouse. Or if days are warm but nights are cool, cover the herbs only at night with burlap or bushel baskets.

You can grow herbs that thrive in cool weather (such as winter scallions, arugula, and mustard) in a cold frame, a glass or plastic enclosed box with a lid you can open for harvesting or ventilation. With this kind of protection, they'll keep growing deep into winter, long after other herbs are gone.

FALL CLEAN-UP

*F*all is the perfect time to tidy up the herb garden and prepare for a new growing season next year. Doing a little garden cleaning and preparation now gives you a pleasant view all winter and a head start next spring. It also reduces the potential for problems with pests and diseases.

Begin by removing old brown stems, but leave stems of woody herbs, unless they're damaged or diseased. They'll resprout in the spring. Be aggressive when you trim (or dig) back spreading herbs such as mint and bee balm — they'll continue to grow during fall and winter.

Dig out any perennial weeds and pull or hoe up annual weeds. Unless the debris is diseased, insect-ridden, or full of seeds, put it in the compost pile. Put problematic material in the garbage or bury it well away from the garden. This gets rid of the overwintering hideouts of many garden pests and problems and so benefits your garden next year.

Early fall can be a good time to rearrange the garden. Move spring- or early summer–flowering herbs by digging up as big a root ball as possible and moving the whole soil-encased ball to the new site. Plant immediately and keep moist.

You can divide hardy perennial herbs now; work on large divisions up to several weeks before the first fall frost or small divisions up to 6 weeks before frost.

If you live where winters are especially cold, you may want to wait until spring to do most of your division or transplanting work. But you can tag the plants now so you'll know where they are and can start early in spring.

Wrap plants that suffer from winter cold and winds with burlap, which also helps prevent them from breaking open under heavy snow or ice. Try this on woody but tender perennials; in warmer climates with dry winter winds, rosemary and other tender evergreens may benefit from being wrapped in burlap.

Horseradish

Horseradish grows prolifically in colder climates and adds plenty of zest to meals. It is easy to propagate by taking root cuttings. You can do this in spring or fall. Cut the roots into sections that are an inch or two long. Another even easier way to get new plants is to take the small plants that crop up from the main root, retaining the crown or top shoots on as many as possible.

Choose an open spot with light and rich soil. Plant each root cutting about 2 inches deep with the crown upright.

Woody but tender perenials may suffer from winter cold and winds. They should be wrapped with burlap to prevent damage under heavy snow or ice.

CHAPTER 9

HERB GARDENING IN WINTER

Your herb activities don't have to come to a screeching halt when winter arrives. You can grow some herbs indoors. Start new seedlings or cuttings while the weather is still mild outdoors. Or dig up the herbs you can't live without and bring them in. The low light levels, cramped spaces, and dry air indoors can be a bit limiting; but if you follow a few special guidelines, you can have a wonderful indoor garden.

Winter Mulch: Pros & Cons

Mulch can be a great help in the herb garden in summer, and it can be handy in winter, too. When temperatures drop in early winter, cover woody, semi-evergreen herbs such as thyme and lavender with pine boughs to protect them from wind and extreme cold.

In areas with well-drained soil, cover firmly frozen soil with a 4- to 6- inch layer of a fluffy mulch such as salt hay or pine boughs. This helps keep the soil stable and frozen, which is easier on hardy plant roots and prevents frost-heaving. It also can increase the chances of survival for marginally hardy plants.

But think twice about using mulch if you have anything less than well-drained soil, live in a climate with very rainy winters, or grow herbs that need very good drainage. If the soil thaws, mulch will keep it moist — which can encourage root rot and other problems. If you live in a climate with extended warm periods during winter, be sure to pull the mulch back away from the plants in warm weather; put it back when the soil refreezes. And remove the mulch promptly in spring when weather moderates. You also should keep an eye out for mice and other small animals that may make a home in the mulch and dine on your herbs.

~

(Opposite page)

A pot of rosemary on the kitchen windowsill provides fresh herb clippings for winter meals.

~

Photo: © Patricia J. Bruno / Positive Images

INDOOR HERB GARDENING

Familiarize yourself with all the elements that affect plant growth. You will have to play Mother Nature and provide all of those elements when you grow herbs indoors.

Be sure that you have a reliable source of light. Most herbs need 5 or 6 hours of direct sun, but a few can make do with indirect sun, if they receive at least 8 hours of it. North-facing windows don't get enough light for herbs. Instead, use south-facing windows, which receive the most sun; if you have no trees or other obstructions you can try east-facing windows, which get morning light, or west-facing windows, which get afternoon light. But relying on sunlight cast through windows can be disappointing. Your plants may not get what they need if you have a wide roof overhang, evergreen trees that block the window, or lots of overcast days. For a reliable light source, consider installing a grow light.

You must also pay a bit more attention to the water and nutrient needs of your indoor plants. Different herbs need different quantities of water when grown indoors. Basil, parsley, mint, chervil, and arugula do best if kept moist, not bone dry or soggy wet. Let Mediterranean plants such as rosemary and lavender dry out slightly before you water again. Adjust the amount you fertilize to your light levels. In a dark area, where herbs struggle to stay alive, they may not need fertilizer at all. In bright light where herbs are actively growing, you can fertilize every month. Be sure to harvest fast-growing herbs often so they'll stay compact. And you may want to replant crops that you use often so you'll always have a fresh young plant to take the place of an older plant.

Provide extra humidity indoors because furnaces can make indoor air crackling dry in the winter. Grow herbs in a slightly damp basement under lights, or put the pots on trays of pebbles, with water in the bottom of the trays. The plants shouldn't sit in water; instead it should evaporate up around them. To reduce problems with fungus diseases, make sure air flows freely around the plants. But don't put them in front of a heating vent; it's too hot and dry there.

Growing Rosemary Indoors

One of the most popular herbs to grow indoors is rosemary. To keep your plant thriving, follow these guidelines from nurseryman Tom DeBaggio. Put your rosemary plant in your sunniest window and allow it to dry out between waterings until it almost wilts. Don't water or mist the plant when the weather is overcast. Without sun, the plant can't use the water and could drown. If the plant is suffocating from too much water, the leaves or leaf tips will turn brown and fall off — let the pot dry out, and quickly. If you see yellowing leaves around the base of the plant, the plant is potbound. Transplant it into a pot that's 3 or 4 inches larger.

Plants for the Indoor Winter Garden

Although bringing in mature plants can be challenging, it is worth the fun of experimenting. Then when you wish it were still summer, spend time nurturing your sage or your lavender. Experiment and learn.

Sow Seed	Take Cuttings	Bring in Mature Plants
Arugula	Basil	Chives
Basil	Mint	Garlic chives
Chervil	Oregano	Greek oregano
Coriander/cilantro	Pineapple sage	Lavender
Dill	Rosemary	Lemon verbena
Mustard	Sage	Mint
Parsley	Scented geranium	Rosemary
Summer savory	Thyme	Sage
Sweet marjoram		Scented geranium
		Summer savory
		Sweet bay
		Sweet marjoram
		Thyme

WINTER DOWN TIME

*T*he snow is 6 inches deep, perfect for skiing but terrible for harvesting. The wind is blowing, bringing with it a below-zero wind chill. Your car ignition is working in slow motion, if it's working at all. You don't feel like venturing out without triple layers of clothing from head to toe.

So don't go out. Use winter down time to plan ahead for the coming year. Reevaluate whether your garden design is really as effective as you'd hoped. Is there something that needs restructuring to make it work better? Are all of your herbs pulling their weight, or do you have some that just don't look or perform as they should? Is there a better plant that could serve as a replacement?

Find out what's new and better among the seed and nursery offerings. Write to the nurseries listed in the appendix of this book for catalogues. You may find the perfect plant for an empty or troubled area of the garden, or you may find one that's perfect for your favorite kind of cooking.

©Patricia J. Bruno / Positive Images

Grow herbs all through the year in decorative containers placed on bright windowsills.

This is a time of new beginnings, so make the most of it and dig into the possibilities.

Take the time to browse through some herb magazines. You can find some new plants to grow, new techniques to use, or new recipes to try. Check at your local library or botanical garden to see what kind of herb magazines are available. If you find one you really like, get a subscription.

Try forcing herbs to grow the old-fashioned way, in a hot bed. Old-time herbalists used to use hot beds to sprout mints, tarragon, and other perennial herbs in midwinter. Set a cold frame or an insulated structure made with walls of straw bales and a top of glass in an open area of the garden. Add a heating cable to warm the hot bed, then plant divisions of mint, tarragon, or another herb you want to experiment with. In a few weeks, the herb may begin to sprout and you'll be the only one in your neighborhood to have homegrown herbs.

You also can make an authentic, manure-heated hot bed. Start with a standard cold frame, but dig out a hollow area 2 feet below. Fill the hollow pit with fresh livestock manure — you can find plenty at any stable. As the manure decomposes, it will release heat that will warm the cold frame. Cover the manure with 4 or 5 inches of well-drained soil and plant your herbs directly in that. You won't even need to use electricity for this ultimate experiment in recycling.

Arugula

PART FOUR

Herb Projects for Every Season

CHAPTER 10

GROWING HERBS IN CONTAINERS

Growing herbs in containers frees you from the clutches of rocky, heavy, or otherwise difficult soil. It lets you use any sunny part of your yard, which is a big help if you're in a yard full of shade trees. It gives you the option of bringing your herbs indoors during winter in cold climates or during summer in steamy or arid climates. Container gardening also lets you create useful and decorative highlights for your window boxes and windowsills, indoor plantscape, patio, deck, front steps — anywhere that a pot of herbs can draw the eye and paint an appealing picture.

Fortunately, many herbs are perfect candidates for growing in containers. This is particularly true of the drought-tolerant herbs — they can make do with less than ideal moisture levels if you forget to water for a day or two. And if you choose your plant combinations wisely, you can create a picture with herbs that's every bit as pretty as with flowers.

The following elements set herb gardening in containers apart from growing herbs in the ground. Keep them in mind as you organize your containers this spring.

CONTAINER TYPES & SIZES

You can choose from a great variety of containers, something to match every kind of plant. If you are looking for a special container — and can't find what you want at your local garden center — it may be in your garden supply catalogue. But when you look for a container, check

~

(Opposite page)

This container full of seasonings features basil, tarragon, parsley, oregano, and thyme.

~

to be sure it has drainage holes at the bottom. If excess rain or water can't escape the pot, it will collect inside and drown the plant.

Consider what the pot is made of and how big it is. That will influence how your herbs will look and how they'll grow. Plastic pots, popular for nurseries because they're easy to use and handle, are lightweight and inexpensive. Air doesn't penetrate through the plastic, so the planting mix won't dry out as quickly as in porous clay pots. In dry seasons or climates, plastic pots can reduce how often you have to water. But on the other hand, clay pots will dry out fairly quickly if overwatered, and plastic pots won't. If you give plants in plastic pots too much water, especially when it's cloudy and cool, you could have problems with soil diseases and damping off.

You can turn leftover nursery pots into herb-growing pots, but to avoid disease problems, wash them out well first with soapy water followed by a dilute bleach solution (1 part bleach to 10 parts water). You also can buy more artistically molded plastic containers that resemble terra-cotta

Herbs in Strawberry Pots

Strawberry pots, upright terra-cotta planters with openings in the sides, are a great way to show off herbs. Fill the side openings with small cascading or bushy herbs to dangle down handsomely — such as sweet marjoram, thyme, lady's mantle, lavender, creeping rosemary, winter savory, oregano, and 'Lemon Gem' marigolds. The opening in the top is a good place for upright and mound-shaped herbs such as parsley, basil, perilla, sage, and lavender, as well as vining ornmentals such as ivy.

Drought-tolerant herbs are clear winners for strawberry pots, because the pots dry out quickly and can be hard to rewet thoroughly. To make watering easier, insert a narrow, perforated plastic tube down the middle of the pot before filling it with soil. You can pour water down the tube and reach all levels of the pot.

As you fill up the container, plant well-rooted seedlings in the holes as you come to them. Insert the root ball slightly below the level of the hole and firm the soil well around it. Once the herb develops a good set of roots, it will prevent much soil from washing out of the hole. Fertilize once a month, or as needed for the herbs you're growing. And be sure to bring the pot indoors in winter in cold climates.

© Rosalind Creasy

Rosemary and thyme are complemented by begonias in this handsomely planted strawberry jar.

pots or have geometric shapes and ornate designs. Decorator plastic pots such as these, unfortunately, are not cheap.

Terra-cotta or clay pots have a pleasant, natural appearance that looks good with most herbs and landscape settings. They are porous; they allow air to penetrate and moisture to evaporate. This feature can be an advantage if you're growing plants like rosemary that suffer from soggy soils, or if you live in a rainy climate. But if you forget to water frequently enough, clay can compound your problem.

Most clay pots are the standard shape, but you can find low dish gardens and other clay shapes if you look hard enough. Clay pots are much heavier than plastic, so they can be harder to move around. But once you get them to their final destination, they tend to stay put, which is good to know if you're growing top-heavy or tall plants, especially in a windy location. Don't leave clay pots outdoors in winter (unless you live in a frost-free climate) or they'll crack.

Glazed, ceramic containers, which tend to be expensive, can turn a potted plant into a piece of art. You can choose from plain pots or ornate patterns and colors in a variety of shapes. But if you spend a good deal on the container, keep it in a safe place where it won't get broken.

Metal buckets, urns, bins, antiques, or fixtures from around the house can double as planters if you make drainage holes in the bottom. Metal containers tend to be weather resistant (although some kinds of metal rust)

To create a hanging basket for herbs using a wire frame, first line the wire with moss. Place a small amount of grower's mix in the basket. Then nestle plants in the moss as shown.

but poorly insulated, so the soil can get very hot or cold depending on the weather.

Wooden crates, half-barrels, and planters make great containers for multiple plantings. But look for untreated, naturally rot-resistant wood, such as cedar and redwood. Some organic gardeners avoid pressure-treated wood because it may leach chemicals into the soil.

Rectangular-shaped trough gardens, low containers crafted out of cement or stone, are great for showcasing miniature herbs and alpine plants. Use one to make a collection of miniature plants such as dittany of Crete, dwarf lavender, dwarf curry plant (*Helichrysum italicum* subsp. *siitalicum* 'Nanum'), miniature lamb's ears, sandwort (*Arenaria montana)*, small dianthus such as 'Pretty Dottie', miniature rosemary, and dwarf oregano.

Hanging baskets are an ideal place to show off herbs that dangle or vine. You can plant your own plastic baskets or buy preplanted hanging baskets at nurseries. You also can make your own moss-lined wire baskets. Fill them with scented geraniums such as 'Mint', 'Apple', 'Coconut', 'Attar of Rose', and 'Snowflake', or creeping rosemary, lavender, thyme, mint, Greek oregano, catmint, sweet marjoram, and creeping winter savory.

Holly Shimizu's Herb Basket Tips

With the following techniques, Holly Shimizu makes massive herb baskets — up to 4 feet across — to display at the U.S. Botanic Garden.

Line a wire basket with 1½ inches of unmilled sphagnum moss. Place a shallow layer of moist potting mix on the moss and you're ready to plant the first tier of seedlings. Shake the seedlings out of their pots, wrap their roots in paper towels, and poke the shoots through holes in the outer moss layer. Leave the roots snug inside. Using this method, set seedlings around the perimeter of the basket. Then add another couple inches of soil and put in another layer of seedlings until the plants reach up to cover the top of the ball. In a month or two, the plants will fill in any open spaces and appear to be a round ball of herbs.

Shimizu has used many different plants in combination: dwarf thyme, prostrate rosemary, dwarf catnip, pendulous flowered oreganos (such as 'Kent Beauty'), and fruit mints. She also plants wire baskets with culinary herbs for a special effect, using, for example, golden lemon thyme, parsley, oregano, and basils.

To keep the basket growing and thriving, Shimizu recommends adding a slow-release fertilizer to the planting mix or watering with an organic blend of fish and kelp fertilizers every 2 to 3 weeks. Cut back the plants as necessary to keep the ball shapely. And be available to water often during the summer.

(Adapted from an article by Holly Shimizu, *Herb Companion*, 1993, vol. 5, no. 5.)

Container Size

Finding a pot of the right size is the key to success when growing any herb in a container. Perhaps you've seen bonsai, miniature trees grown in small pots. The small container size combined with judicious pruning keeps even normal-sized trees to a fraction of their ordinary size. But maintaining them is a skilled art form. For those of us untrained in this beautiful Oriental art, cramping herbs into tiny pots usually ends in disaster. Just imagine how marigolds look when they've been abandoned in a small six-pack too long. They become scraggly and threadbare — not a look that you'd show off.

The problem with small containers is that plants quickly become pot-bound. Their roots grow through all the available planting mix, and then they begin to wind around the perimeter of the pot. They become tangled up in knots, which limits their effectiveness and causes plant health to decline. Of course, just as with bonsai trees, there are ways to avoid growing a struggling root-bound plant. Start with a spacious pot. When the roots fill up the containers, you have two options. You can uproot the plant, divide it or trim the roots and shoots back by one-third, and repot

An ideal container for herb plants is one that allows excess water to drain off. Decorative containers are available at garden centers and nurseries, department stores, and mail-order suppliers.

© Kevin Kennefick

When choosing what size pot a plant will need, keep in mind the spread and depth of the root system.

in the same container in fresh soil. Or you can move the plant up to a larger pot of fresh soil.

But how big is big enough? Consider how deeply the plant's roots grow. Dill, which has a taproot like a carrot, needs a pot at least 8 inches deep. Thyme, which has a more shallow and adaptable fibrous network of roots, can make do in a pot about 4 inches deep.

Pot width also plays an important role. If you want to keep a young plant in a pot for a month or two before planting it in the garden, you can use a narrower container. If you have a healthy year-old perennial herb, you can probably keep it going for another season in an 8-inch-wide nursery container. But if you want to grow a large perennial plant — such as a bay tree or rosemary shrub — permanently in a container, you may eventually have to upgrade the container to a half-barrel size.

To help you calculate the size of container you'll need, carefully dig a one-year-old plant out of the garden in the fall. (Choose one you want to pot up and bring inside.) Try to keep the roots intact so you can see how far the roots have grown over the past summer. Take note of the root spread and depth, and try to find a pot that can accommodate both dimensions.

Container Size Suggestions

Here are some different sizes of pots for different kinds of herbs:

4-inch Pot. Small thyme division, basil seedling, young salad burnet plant, sweet marjoram seedling, or any young nursery plants intended for transplanting.

6-inch Pot. Bush basil, chives, parsley, lamb's ears, sweet marjoram, oregano, thyme, summer savory, sorrel. Note that most herbs won't stay in a 6-inch pot more than 6 to 8 months. Be prepared to transplant perennial herbs into larger containers as necessary.

8-inch Pot. Sweet basil, scented marigolds, dill, lady's mantle, sage, artemisia.

12-inch Pot. Scented geranium, catmint, bronze fennel, lavender, mints, young lemon verbena.

Larger Pots. Mature rosemary, bay tree, lemon verbena.

Growing Medium

Most herb nurseries grow potted plants in synthetic growing mixes — which contain no soil at all. That's because unsterilized garden soil can carry diseases and pests that attack young plants. Garden soil can also pack down in a container, becoming difficult for roots or water to penetrate.

Growing mixes are a useful alternative to garden soil. They blend sphagnum peat moss with vermiculite, perlite, and sometimes charcoal or composted pine bark. The blend is sterile, light and airy, well drained, and hard to overwater. But it's also almost devoid of nutrients (unless enriched with a slow-release fertilizer or compost) and hard to rewet when it gets dry. Because of the high peat moss content, the pH tends to be acidic, although it can change if you water with alkaline water.

Anatomy of a Soilless Mix

Here are the origin and function of the elements that make up soilless mixes:

Peat Moss. This is the primary component of soilless mixes. Peat moss spreads in thick mats over acidic bogs and has a low pH, from 3.5 to 5, which is modified by adding limestone or another buffer in most commercial mixes. It holds water well but is hard to saturate thoroughly when dry, which is a major disadvantage for herbs growing in the summer. Peat helps suppress some diseases, which is in its favor. Some gardeners are concerned about the environmental effect of mining peat moss because peat bogs take centuries to develop. Gerry Hood, president of the Canadian Sphagnum Peat Moss Association, counters by saying that peat harvesting affects very few bogs. (Only 749,000 metric tons of peat are harvested each year, whereas an estimated 50 million tons or more of new peat accumulate each year, he claims.) And the harvested bogs can be reclaimed with proper site management, according to a North American Wetlands Council report on peat mining (partially financed by the Canadian Sphagnum Peat Moss Association). Environmentally sensitive harvesting and reclaiming methods will become the new focus for the Peat Association, Hood pledges.

Meanwhile, you need to use your judgment here — peat moss is vital in soilless mixes.

Vermiculite. This is a form of the mineral mica, heated until it pops into layered sheets. It encourages water drainage but can also hold moisture and nutrients such as compost.

Perlite. This is a volcanic mineral shaped into puffy, white balls that encourage rapid water drainage but won't hold nutrients. Because it's lightweight, perlite sometimes slips up to the top of the pot where it isn't particularly effective.

Charcoal. Small bits of charcoal also encourage better water drainage.

Composted Pine Bark. This is organic matter that holds moisture and nutrients and encourages good drainage. Better yet, it encourages beneficial microbes that discourage root rot and other soilborne diseases.

Compost. The decayed remains of vegetation or livestock manure hold moisture and release gentle quantities of nutrients that nourish plants. Like composted pine bark and peat moss, it, too, can discourage plant diseases.

Once herbs are past the delicate seedling stage, I like to plant them in a mix of 1 part compost for each 2 parts growing mix. This enriches the mix, gives it some weight as well as water- and nutrient-holding capacity, and doesn't hinder the good drainage and aeration. You also can add wetting agents to keep the peat moss moist longer and make it easier to rewet when dry.

Protecting Herbs during the Winter Months

To increase chances of winter survival of hardy perennials in cold climates, sink pots in a well-drained bed or cold frame. Or move them to a cool, but protected, place such as an enclosed, unheated porch or breezeway where the pot won't freeze all the way through. Water occasionally so the potting mix doesn't dry out completely, and watch out for rodents, especially in the winter.

You can also bring container-grown plants indoors for the winter. This gives you a chance to harvest the foliage that remains or to keep herbs of questionable winter hardiness alive for another growing season. Give hardy or marginally hardy herbs such as Greek oregano, French thyme, rosemary, lemon verbena, and lavender a cool location with bright light (at least 5 hours of sun a day or 14 to 16 hours of fluorescent light a day) and fairly humid air. Tender annuals such as basil and sweet marjoram will take normal household temperatures, combined with bright light and reasonable humidity.

TEMPERATURE

Containers, especially if they're small or made out of plastic or metal, feel the full force of daily or seasonal temperature changes. They don't have an insulating blanket of soil or clay around them, and that can make growing difficult for temperature-sensitive herbs. When growing herbs in containers, don't be surprised if your coriander or mustard bolts a little sooner in spring or your lady's mantle develops crisped edges in summer. Even hardy perennial herbs may freeze out in winter.

You can help prevent problems caused by lack of insulation. Whenever possible, plant in large containers. Or group several containers together and fill in between them with decorative sheet moss, leaves, or bark mulch. Put smaller containers inside larger ones and fill the gap between them with moist vermiculite (which also slows down moisture loss). Use light-colored, heat-reflective containers during the heat of summer and darker pots for cool times in spring and fall.

LIGHT EXPOSURE

Usually container-grown plants need the same amount of light that you would give garden-grown plants, especially when temperatures are moderate. But in the heat of summer, you may want to place container plants where they'll have light shade during the afternoon.

WATERING

You'll have to tend container-grown herbs more carefully than those that grow in a garden bed. Here's how. Water whenever the soil begins to dry out. Stick your finger an inch or two deep into the planting mix. If it's dry down there, it's time to water. Another way to tell if the mix in a plastic pot is dry is to lift the plant. If it feels especially light, it's time to water.

In the summer you might need to water plants once or twice a day. But during winter, herbs need much less moisture. Be especially careful not to overwater plants that need excellent drainage, such as rosemary and lavender. Tom DeBaggio lets the soil in a pot of rosemary dry out until the plant almost wilts before he waters again (especially if it's in a plastic pot). If you are keeping your rosemary indoors in winter and it takes longer than a week to let this dry, DeBaggio says you can turn a fan on the plant to help the soil dry out.

The exact watering schedule you need to follow depends on several factors: plant selection, pot size and make, and weather. Drought-tolerant herbs tolerate longer gaps between watering than water-loving herbs such as mint. Tightly planted pots, or those situated in hot, sunny, and dry locations, will need watering more frequently. Smaller pots will dry out in the wink of an eye and may need a thorough soaking as often as twice a day. Larger pots might only need watering every couple days in the summer, less in the spring, winter, and fall.

When you do water, be sure to soak the soil until the water runs out the bottom of the pot. Dump out any excess water that may pool in the saucer. If white salts collect on the soil surface or sides of a clay pot, submerge the pot in a tub of water for a few minutes to dissolve the salts and wash them away. If you let salts build up, they can burn the plant roots.

FERTILIZER

When you plant in a peat-based mix, even one amended with compost, you'll need to provide extra fertilizer. Most commercial growing mixes contain a small amount of fertilizer to get plants started. But it is quickly depleted, and then plants will grow stunted, off-color,

© Rosalind Creasy

When the seasonal temperatures allow for it, containers of herbs can be moved outside to enhance walkways or paths — wherever they can be seen and enjoyed.

and unhealthy. For a gentle trickle of nutrients, use a balanced, slow-release solid fertilizer such as compost, kelp meal, dried manures, or a packaged, slow-release organic blend. Alternatively, you can water regularly with half-strength, water-soluble fertilizers such as compost tea, fish emulsion, or liquid kelp.

Keep an eye on the soil pH. If it gets excessively acid or alkaline, it will limit nutrient availability. To make a potting mix less acidic, add ground oyster shells or limestone. If it becomes too alkaline, add powdered sulfur or peat moss. Follow the directions on the label carefully so you don't do more harm than good when making pH adjustments.

COMBINING PLANTS IN CONTAINERS

*T*he previous pointers will help you grow individual plants in pots, but you also can combine several herbs in one planter. To get a better feel for combination planters, let's compare them to a small house full of relatives for a holiday weekend. If everyone gets along, the cramped situation can be quite enjoyable. But if even one person clashes with the others, it can dampen the festivities for everyone. Herbs grown in containers are in similar tight quarters. They snuggle side by side, sharing rooting and growing space. This can be a wonderful situation if the herbs are compatible, but it can be disappointing if even one plant is too aggressive or overcrowded. Here are some criteria you need to consider to be sure the container garden will grow smoothly.

- Determine the mature size of each herb and work out your spacing from that. Remember, seeds and seedlings may look small at first, but they'll grow.

- Find different species that can share the soil and sun. Combine shallow- and deep-rooted plants in a deep pot; put tall, sun-loving plants with low-growing, shade-tolerant plants. This creates harmony and allows both kinds of plants to grow well and flourish.

© Rosalind Creasy

This strawberry pot spills over with purple sage and garlic chives.

Some Container Combinations

Here are some herb combination ideas to whet your creative appetites:

Spring Basket for Shade: Violets and sweet woodruff

Italian Specialty Planter: Italian paprika peppers and Greek oregano

Potted Purple and Gold: Giant red mustard (*Brassica juncea* var. *rugosa*, a salad plant) and lady's mantle in spring; replace the mustard with 'Opal' basil in summer and remove faded flowers on lady's mantle for repeated blooming.

Golden Glow: Golden 'Icterina' sage, dill, curly leaf parsley, and golden lemon thyme

Pot of Silver: Lavender with silver thyme and 'Silver Mound' artemisia

White Highlights: 'Snowflake' scented geranium with lamb's ears

Blue and Bronze Planter: Catmint with bronze fennel

Purple Highlights: 'Purple Ruffles' basil, chives, and 'Tricolor' sage

- Consider the growing conditions required by each herb. In a sunny dry spot, use sun-loving and heat- and drought-tolerant plants. In cool, shady spots, use spring-blooming or shade-loving herbs.

- Pick a color scheme and stick to it. Use herbs with colorful foliage and add a few flowers too.

- Develop a sequence of bloom with herbs that flower early, midseason, and late.

- Choose herbs that fit a particular theme that strikes your interest — for instance, a planter of pizza herbs or sweetly scented herbs.

RECIPES & CRAFTS

*I*n the spring, you started herbs indoors. Later you put your seedlings in the garden you carefully designed, where they flourished under your loving care. Toward fall, you potted up herbs and brought them indoors for the winter. Other herbs you harvested, drying them or freezing them.

But the pleasure these herbs gave you in the growing season doesn't end with first frost. With containers of herbs in your house through the winter, you can conceivably grow herbs all year. Therefore you can use them all year long, too. Or if you have dried or frozen them, herbs are available for use anytime. This chapter will give you instructions on preserving herbs, herb recipe ideas, craft projects, and suggestions for using herbs in dozens of different ways. The possibilities are as extensive as your imagination. The recipes and crafts given here can get you started, but I think you will find that there are no limits to the ways you can enjoy herbs — all year long.

PRESERVING HERBS

*W*hich method should you choose? Dried herbs have concentrated flavor that is delightful to use. Some home-dried herbs are so aromatic that they perfume the entire kitchen when you open the jar and crush them in a dish. Others are wonderful for fragrant potpourri that will fill the house with the smell of springtime.

Here's a quick checklist of good ways to preserve the herbs you are growing:

- Drying works well for basil, dill, fennel, lovage, mint, oregano, parsley, hot peppers, rosemary, sage, savory, scented geraniums, tarragon, and thyme.

- Freezing works well with basil, chervil, chives, cilantro, dill, lemon balm, parsley, hot peppers, sorrel, sweet cicely, and tarragon.

~

(Opposite page)
**Artemisia is laid flat
to dry for a variety
of craft projects.**

~

Photo: © William D. Adams

153

How to Dry Herbs

To dry thin-leaved herbs such as thyme and rosemary, make bundles of 3 to 5 sprigs, tie them together with a twist tie, and hang them in a warm, airy, dry, and dark location. (Keep them out of the traffic areas.) If you live in an area with high humidity, dry herbs in an air-conditioned room. If you need extra warmth for good drying, put them in a gas oven with a pilot light. They should dry to feel crisp in a couple days.

For large-leaved herbs you can't get to dry well by hanging (as in the humid dog-days of August), buy a dehydrator. Any dehydrator will work as long as it has a low setting (90°–95°F) for herbs. You can put sprigs or individual leaves in the dehydrator. The leaves will dry faster when stripped off the stem, but sprigs are easier to handle. When dried, the crispy leaves snap right off when you run your fingers down the stem. Most herbs will dry overnight in a dehydrator.

When the herbs are dry, put them in the oven at 120°F for a few minutes to make the herbs as crackly as corn flakes. Strip the leaves off the

© David Cavagnaro

Take your drying tray right into the garden and lay out lengths of spearmint to dry for tea.

Nutritional Value of Herbs

The foliage of many herbs can contribute some minerals to your diet, but herb seeds or fruits are often better sources of vitamins. For example, fresh borage leaves contain potassium, calcium, and other minerals. Chile peppers are full of vitamins C, A, E, and B_1 thiamine.

The following list gives the nutritional value of a selection of herbs.

Basil, 1 t.	131 IU Vitamin A, 48 mg K
Cayenne pepper, 1 t.	749 IU Vitamin A, 36 mg K, .14 mg Fe
Celery seed, 1 t.	.4 g protein, 35 mg Ca, 11 mg P, 28 mg K
Dill seed, dried, 1 t.	25 mg K, 32 mg Ca, .34 mg Fe
Dill weed, dried, 1 t.	33 mg K, .49 mg Fe, 18 mg Ca
Fennel seed, 1 t.	34 mg Na, 10 mg Ca, .37 mg Mg
Marjoram, dried, 1 t.	48 IU Vitamin A, .5 mg Fe
Oregano, ground, 1 t.	104 IU Vitamin A, 25 mg K, 24 mg Ca, .66 mg Fe
Paprika, 1 t.	1273 IU Vitamin A, 49 mg K, .50 mg Fe
Parsley, dried, 1 t.	303 IU Vitamin A, 49 mg K, 1.27 mg Fe, 19 mg Ca
Sage, ground, 1 t.	41 IU Vitamin A, .20 mg Fe
Tarragon, ground, 1 t.	67 IU Vitamin A, 48 mg K, 18 mg Ca

US Recommended Daily Allowance for Adults and Children over Age 4

Vitamin A	5000 IU
Calcium (Ca)	1.0 g
Iron (Fe)	18 mg
Magnesium (Mg)	400 mg

Source: Jean A.T. Pennington, *Food Values*, New York: Harper & Row, 1989.
K = potassium, Ca = calcium, P = phosphorus, Fe = iron, Na = sodium, Mg = magnesium.

One way to gather dill seed is to hang the plant upside-down and wrap a paper bag around it to collect the seed as it dries and falls off.

woody stems. If you're sure they're completely dry, you can store the whole leaves, which helps preserve essential oils. But I've had a lot of problems with mildew on herbs stored this way. So I now process them into flakes in a blender or food processor. I add a cup or two of leaves and pulse them in the blender until they become large flakes. Then I seal them in an airtight jar. I like to add a small packet of white rice, wrapped up in cloth or paper, to suck up any excess humidity. You can store the jars in a cool, dark cupboard, but I like to keep the jars in the refrigerator, which helps preserve quality longer.

To dry roots such as orris root, horseradish, and lovage, slice them thin and put them in a dehydrator or warm oven to dry until they are hard. Store in an airtight jar.

To dry seeds, hang the mature plants upside-down over newspaper or cloth in a warm, dry location. When the seeds fall, they're easy to scoop up. You also can dry herb seeds in a dehydrator on low heat. But if the seeds are small, cover the drying trays with cheesecloth so the seeds won't fall through. When dry, you may need to separate the seeds from the rest of

Substituting Dried for Fresh Herbs

You can substitute dried herbs for fresh using 1 teaspoon of dried herbs instead of 2 to 3 teaspoons of fresh herbs. If the dried herb is very fresh and aromatic, use a smaller amount. If it has lost some flavor, use a larger amount.

the plant. Put the dried material on one side of a cookie sheet that has elevated edges. Crush the plant debris with a coffee cup or your hands. Then elevate the tray slightly so the seeds will slide down, separate from the chaff. Once they are separated, put the seeds in the freezer for 48 hours to kill any pests that may be inside. Then seal them in an airtight jar and store in a cool, dry location.

To dry flowers for potpourri or herb wreaths, place individual flowers or sprigs in the dehydrator. Grower Marty Sickinger likes to dry flowers upright in a vase with a little bit of water. Let the water evaporate slowly, while the plants maintain their open shape. This works especially well with black-eyed Susans and daffodils, which would dry closed up if you hung them upside-down. Experiment with different flowers. Some dry well upside-down, and some dry best spread out on a screen. Develop the method that works best for you.

How to Freeze Herbs

Some herbs such as chervil, cilantro, and lemon balm lose much of their aroma when dried. Dried sage loses much of its sweetness and becomes harsher flavored. Fleshy-leaved herbs dried in humid weather without a dehydrator may mildew and become worthless.

This is why some herb enthusiasts say that freezing is the best way to preserve herbs — it conserves the delicate essential oils that are lost when herbs are heated. Freezing captures harvest-fresh flavor but usually sacrifices texture. Basil, for instance, turns black and mushy; it's not particularly pleasant to handle but still flavorful. So use it and other frozen herbs in cooked dishes or purees where the limp texture won't be offensive. Handle the herbs while they're frozen, and they'll still feel firm. Or blend fresh herbs with oil into a concentrated herb paste.

Freeze herbs whole. To freeze herbs whole, wash and pat them dry. Then pack them in freezer bags in a mass. To use, slice off a chunk, chop it up, and drop it in your spaghetti sauce or casserole.

Freeze individual leaves or stems. Lay individual leaves or stems on a cookie sheet to freeze individually and then pack in a freezer container. You can pull out a leaf at a time as you need it.

Mince herbs and freeze them in water in an ice cube tray. They are ready to drop into soups or stews with no further fuss.

Make herbs into paste to freeze. This is an excellent way to freeze herbs and is highly recommended by Madelene Hill. Puree them or chop them with oil, somewhat like pesto but without the extra garlic, cheese, and nuts. The flavor blends into the oil, and the oil becomes a barrier that protects the herbs from freezing, thawing, or drying out in freezer conditions, thus preserving their fresh flavor and color. This is an especially good way to use an herb such as dill that is only in the garden for a short time. Freezing it in a paste gives you fresh dill flavor year-round.

Use your food processor to make a concentrated paste of herbs without a lot of oil. You can use a blender if it is powerful and you add more oil and stir more frequently. Use ½ cup vegetable oil to 2 cups hard-packed leaves. Some people prefer olive oil, but it is expensive and you might not want olive oil flavor in every dish you make. Canola and other vegetable oils are much less expensive.

Pack the paste into airtight, freezer-safe containers, label, date them, and freeze them immediately to avoid the risk of botulism. (Refrigeration isn't good enough to be safe.) You can use the paste like dried herbs; it ends up with a flavor about three times as strong as fresh herbs. And, it's super convenient. The oils don't freeze solid, so you can just cut off what you need with a paring knife.

For other preserving ideas, consider Pestos and Herb Sugars, Herb Vinegars, Herb Salts, Herb Cheese and Butters, and Culinary Mixes (later in this chapter).

HERBAL MIXTURES

In addition to saving herbs separately, mix some ready-to-use blends that you can sprinkle into anything you are making. It's great to grow your own herbs but even better to be able to use them all the time with no extra work.

Chop up fresh herbs, blend them with others, and seal them in individual, serving-size containers in the freezer. Or dry them, pulse them into flakes in the food processor or blender, and combine them with others in an airtight jar. You can just dip in a measuring spoon and sprinkle as much as you need into whatever you are making. Keep a couple of different blends around your kitchen.

Fines Herbes

Fines herbes is a mild-flavored blend of equal parts of chives, parsley, and chervil. It is good in eggs or cheese dishes, and other foods. You can also add up to three other herbs such as thyme, savory, tarragon, sweet marjoram, or Greek oregano. It is most common to use this blend fresh and to add it in the final minutes of cooking. But you can freeze the extra for later and use it as you would fresh. You can also make fines herbes out of dried herbs and add them slightly earlier in the cooking process.

A mortar and pestle can be useful for grinding dried herbs into flakes or a fine powder.

Salting Herbs

You can dry herbs in salt and use the flavored salt to season your foods. Salt draws moisture from herbs and at the same time absorbs some of their essential oils. It works best with thin-leaved herbs such as savory, rosemary, marjoram, dill, tarragon, and thyme, but it can be satisfactory with most large-leaved herbs such as basil if you use fewer leaves and more salt. Here is how you dry herbs in salt.

Harvest the herbs you want to use, either a single type or a blend of complementary herbs. Wash them and dry them well with a thick towel. Then remove any thick stems or inedible parts. Chop the herbs up finely if you intend to use the salt and herb blend directly for seasoning. Now take a container of non-iodized or kosher salt and an airtight container such as a canning jar or freezer container. Put a ¼-inch layer of salt in the bottom. Then sprinkle on a thin layer of herbs. Cover the herbs with another layer of salt, and continue in this manner until you have used up all your herbs or reached the top of the container. Cover the top layer of herbs completely with salt and seal the jar.

In about a week, the herbs will be dry. You can pull out individual sprigs and crumble them into dishes as they are. Or you can brush off the extra salt before you use them. If you want to use the herbed salt to sprinkle on a variety of foods, blend the herbs together with the salt thoroughly. Then pour into a smaller, airtight container that you can keep on your kitchen counter or dining room table.

Bouquet Garni

Bouquet garni is a mix of herbs used to flavor stews, soups, braised dishes, and other liquid-based foods. You can place the herbs in a tea ball, tie herb sprigs together at the base of the stem, or enclose dried or minced fresh or frozen herbs in a little bag of cheesecloth. Put the herbs in the dish during the last 30 minutes of heating. Pull them out when your food is done cooking, leaving only the flavor behind. You can adapt the blend of herbs according to what you are cooking. But traditionally, bouquet garni includes generous portions of parsley, sweet bay, thyme, and lovage or celery leaves.

Sample Seasoning Blends

Here are herb blends that make the most of different kinds of food. Experiment with them to find your own perfect blend. If you like strongly flavored foods, go heavier on the garlic and bolder-flavored herbs. If you like more subtle seasonings, go heavier on milder herbs such as parsley and lemon thyme.

- *Chicken Seasoning:* dried garlic, tarragon, and lemon thyme
- *Italian Seasoning:* oregano, marjoram, basil, and thyme

- *Herbed Mayonnaise Seasoning:* basil, dill, or tarragon
- *Popcorn Seasoning:* chile powder, garlic, and parsley (put these herbs in the cooking oil or sprinkle on after popping in microwave or air-popper)
- *Salt-Free Herb Blend I:* lovage, parsley, dill, lemon zest (grated yellow part of lemon rind)
- *Salt-Free Herb Blend II:* dill, grated ginger root, chopped garlic

HERBAL VINEGARS

Long before our ancestors had refrigerators, they preserved their herbs by dunking them in a bottle of wine or vinegar. It was a surprisingly effective way to capture the fresh flavor of the herbs and to make herbs even more useful in medicine and cuisine. Today, you can use herbal vinegars in salad dressings (mixed with oil or yogurt), sauces,

© Lee Ann White / Positive Images

Several different kinds of basil are among the herbs popularly used to flavor vinegars.

Peppermint

Salad

⅓ cup chopped hazelnuts

2 quarts mixed lettuces torn into bite-sized pieces

1 cup loosely packed fresh mint leaves

¼ cup Italian parsley leaves

1 cup loosely packed green basil leaves

¼ cup thinly sliced scallions

2 fresh peaches, peeled and sliced, or 2 cups sliced fresh strawberries

Make the dressing by combining 2 T. raspberry vinegar, 2 T. orange juice, 1 t. dijon mustard, salt and pepper. Gradually add 3 T. olive oil and 3 T. salad oil, whisking until blended. In a large salad bowl, combine greens and fruit. Pour dressing over salad and toss lightly.

Yield: Serves 4 to 6   *Raboff & Renée Shepherd*

SAVORY CHEESES & BUTTERS

You can also use the herbs you grew to make wonderful seasoned herb butters and cheeses. You can use herb butters in or on breakfast breads, rolls, French bread, over vegetables, pasta, rice, grilled meats, casseroles, stir-fries — anywhere you would ordinarily use butter or margarine. Herbal cheeses are more like party foods, hors d'oeuvres to serve with crackers or toast. But you can also use them to make everyday foods like cheese sandwiches special.

To make, wash fresh herbs and pat them dry. Chop them finely, add a bit of lemon juice, and mix into soft, room-temperature butter, margarine, or cheese. If the cheese is too firm, blend it with some yogurt or cream cheese. You can mix the butters and cheeses with the herbs by hand (if you grate the hard cheese first) or puree them together in the food processor. You can also form the cheese into small balls and roll it in herbs, combined with nuts and oil if you wish. Refrigerate butters and cheeses for a few hours, at least, so the flavors can mix. You can also freeze herb butters for a couple of months.

Herbal Combinations to Flavor Butter

Here are some great combinations for you to mix and match in butter or margarine.

Full-Flavored Butters for Lamb or Beans. Rosemary or winter savory

Grilled Meat Blend. Combine garlic, thyme, and sweet marjoram (baste on grilling meats)

Chicken or Fish Butters. Combine fennel or tarragon with dill

All-Purpose Butter. Parsley, marjoram, thyme, basil, and a bit of garlic

Just-the-Basics Butter. Chives and dill

Herb Butter

½ cup butter (1 stick), softened

1 sprig finely snipped fresh thyme

2 tablespoons chopped fresh parsley

1 clove garlic, finely minced

1 sprig finely snipped oregano

2 teaspoons finely chopped chives

2 teaspoons grated lemon peel

Beat butter until fluffy. Mix in remaining ingredients. Chill several hours to blend flavors. Use on warm bread, cooked fresh vegetables (such as peas, green beans, or broccoli), or grilled seafood.

Yield: ½ cup (enough for 1 loaf of French bread)   *Millie Adams*

Stuffed Nasturtium Flowers

24 nasturtium flowers

4 ounces cream cheese, softened

2 ounces butter, softened

½ teaspoon lemon juice

½ teaspoon sugar

¼ teaspoon white pepper

1 clove garlic, minced

Mix cream cheese, butter, lemon juice, sugar, pepper, and garlic until well blended. Place cream cheese mixture in a pastry bag fitted with a round tip. Carefully fill each nasturtium flower with about 1 teaspoon of the mixture. Serve immediately.

Yield: Serves 4 to 6 as an appetizer   *Lori Zaim*

PESTO

*Y*ou can turn most herbs into pesto, an herb and oil paste flavored with nuts, garlic, and Parmesan cheese. There are two advantages to making pesto. You can use both herb leaves and the soft stems. And you can freeze pesto to make a quick and delicious meal any time.

Pesto is great on pasta and in dressings, casseroles, or stir-fries. Blend pesto with oil and vinegar to douse on salads or submarine sandwiches, add it to mayonnaise for chicken or tuna salad, or drizzle it over chicken roasted without the skin. If you have extra, freeze it in quarter-cup servings so it's easy to plug into recipes when you need it. Let the frozen pesto thaw in the refrigerator for a couple of hours to add to cold food. Or to serve it warm, drop frozen pesto into hot dishes during the last few minutes of cooking.

To make pesto you'll need a food processor — most blenders aren't powerful enough to puree herbs. Read your food processor instruction booklet for operating details. Then gather 2 cups of your fresh herbs of choice. Herbs that work well include basil, chives, coriander, dill, French tarragon, chervil, jalapeno peppers, lovage, sweet marjoram, mint, garlic, sage, rosemary, or tarragon. Place in a food processor with a couple cloves of garlic, ¾ cup cheese (Parmesan is good), and about ¼ cup of nuts (experiment with your favorite raw nuts); pulse to chop the herbs. Keep the blades spinning while you drizzle in about ½ cup canola or olive oil and process until the pesto becomes a smooth paste.

Roasted Garlic

Brush peeled garlic cloves with vegetable oil and bake at 325°F for 25 minutes or until they are tender. Turn once or twice while baking. Season with salt and freshly ground pepper if you wish.

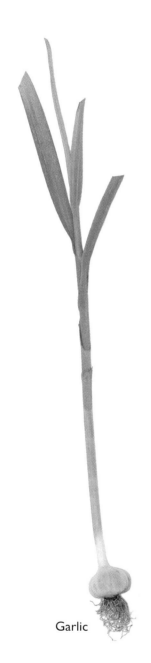

Garlic

Cilantro Pesto

1½ cups cilantro

⅓ cup pine nuts

¼ cup grated Asiago cheese

1 tablespoon lemon juice

¼ to ⅓ cup olive oil

Salt, pepper

Dash dried smoked chipotle chiles

Combine cilantro, nuts, cheese, and lemon juice in food processor or blender. Add olive oil, a little at a time, processing until smooth. Season with salt and pepper to taste. Add chiles. Refrigerate until ready to use.

Karen Small and Cyndi Spresser
Jezebel's, Chagrin Falls, Ohio

Chive Pesto

1 large clove of garlic

3 ounces Parmesan cheese (⅔ cup)

1 cup fresh snipped chives

1 cup flat leaf parsley

¼ cup pine nuts

1 teaspoon salt

1 cup olive oil, preferably extra virgin

Toast the pine nuts in a dry skillet over medium heat, stirring constantly until lightly browned, about 5 minutes.

Mince the garlic clove with a food processor. Place the cheese, chives, parsley, nuts, and salt into the bowl of the food processor. Mince them by pulsing the machine about 8 times. With the food processor running, slowly pour the oil through the feed tube in a steady stream until the mixture is well blended.

Serving Suggestions: *Toss with pasta for a side dish or light main course.*

Or mix ⅔ cup pesto with ⅓ cup mayonnaise to make a delicious dressing for pasta salad. Top the salad with Parmesan cheese and a sprinkling of freshly ground black pepper.

Or flatten boneless chicken breast halves with a wooden mallet. Spread a layer of pesto on each breast. Roll the breasts up to enclose the pesto and wrap firmly in aluminum foil. Cook the foil parcels at 350°F for 40 minutes. Either serve hot or allow to cool and slice when nearly cool.

Yield: About 1½ cups

Lori Zaim

Sweet Herbs: Herb Sugars & Crystallized Herbs

*M*adelene Hill preserves the flavors of some of the sweeter herbs in sugar. The flavors blend and make lovely, subtle combinations to use instead of regular sugar in any cold food. Rose and lemon-scented geraniums, lemon verbena, or orange and lemon zest are particularly good to use in herb sugars.

You can pack fresh herb leaves in granulated white sugar in airtight containers. Stir every day to prevent clumping. After the sugar stays dry and loose, remove the leaves before they become crumbly, and use the finished "herb sugar" in iced teas or desserts. Note: The aromatic oils bake off, so they don't work well in baked or cooked dishes.

To make herbs into syrups to add to iced tea or lemonade or bake into custards or other desserts, Madelene Hill recommends putting a handful of herb branches in a simmering sugar syrup; remove them when the herbs lose their color and the syrup is fragrant. The syrup is ready to use right away.

American colonists, who couldn't run to the store to buy candy when they had a sweet tooth, made their own sweet treats out of herbs. They candied young angelica stems and ginger, preserving the herb and bringing out its flavor with a crystal sugar shell. Although these may not replace modern candies, they are wonderful to use as dessert garnishes or edible decorations on cakes and pastries.

Cookbooks of the 1700s recommended this process for candied angelica. Harvest young angelica stems and boil them until tender. Peel off the fibrous strings and simmer the stems again until they become very green. Dry the stems and weigh them; add a pound of double-refined (very finely textured) sugar to each pound of angelica stems. Let the combination stand for two days, then boil the blend until it becomes clear. Drain off the syrup. Spread another pound of refined sugar over the angelica, set the stems on glass plates, and let them dry in a warm place.

Violets and rose petals are even easier to candy. Brush a little egg white all over each flower and dip it in superfine or powdered sugar. Let the sugar dry into a clear coating, and store in an airtight container.

Angelica

Use fresh mint sprigs to garnish a cup of tea.

BREWING THE BEST TEAS

*A*ny time of the year is a fine time to get into the tea spirit. Collect the herbs you will need and begin to experiment with different brews. Once your favorite recipes are perfected, you can enjoy them all winter. You can also use them for iced tea in summer if you double the concentration of herbs.

In my experiments with homemade herb teas, especially when comparing them to commercial herb teas, I have found that herb teas can be so mild that they may not taste like much. That is because some herbs, such as lemon balm, are best when used fresh. You will be disappointed if you try them dried. You should also know that other herbs, such as pineapple sage, many scented geraniums, and bee balm, have more aroma than

Herbs that Repel Moths

Cedar (shavings)	Mints
English pennyroyal	Rosemary
Eucalyptus	Rue
Gray and green santolina	Southernwood
	Tansy
Lavender	Thyme
Lemon geranium	Wormwood

Mix everything together, close the lid, and let the aromas blend for a few days. At this point you can add a few drops of an essential oil if the aroma is not fragrant enough for you. After a couple of weeks, take out any amount of potpourri you need, and store the rest in the airtight bowl in a cool, dark place. When the potpourri aroma begins to fade, refresh it with a few more drops of essential oil or replace the mixture with fresh potpourri from the sealed container.

If the blend you make isn't immediately to your liking, seal it up for a few months to let the aromas mellow. Or you can neutralize the fragrances with dried lemon, or orange peels or citrus oils.

If you want to make sachets instead of potpourri, it is not necessary to include colorful flowers. Instead, package the herb mix in a pretty cloth bag and tie the top with ribbon. Put the bag in your dresser to scent your clothes.

Ingredients for Potpourri

Here is a list of fragrant herbs and other good scents that you can mix into potpourris.

Fixatives:
Orris root (*Iris* x *germanica* var. *florentina*), calamus root (*Acorus calamus*), storax (*Liquidambar orientalis*), gum benzoin (*Styrax benzoin*), frankincense, myrrh, and others. Use fixatives (especially orris root) in chunk form rather than powdered form; powders will make your potpourri look dusty.

Spices:
Nutmeg, cloves, cinnamon, mace, allspice, anise, cardamom, cedar shavings, sandalwood shavings, angelica root, crushed vanilla beans, and dried lemon or orange peel. Use whole spices or chunks; ground spices can look like dirt in potpourri.

Herbs:
Lavender, lemon verbena, sweet bay, rosemary, cinnamon, licorice or holy basil, angelica, scented geraniums, thyme, pineapple sage, tarragon, basil, sweet marjoram, rosemary, mints, anise seeds, coriander seeds, and bee balm.

Flowers:
Rose buds and petals, bee balm, borage, most herb flowers (including those from mint, thyme, and basil), yarrow, calendula petals, lamb's ears, and pineapple sage. You can also use garden flowers such as marigolds, bachelor's-button, and everlastings — most anything will do as long as it is colorful and nontoxic. (If you have young children who might sample open dishes of potpourri, avoid poisonous flowers such as delphiniums, monkshood, foxglove, and lily of the valley.)

Essential Oils:
These are the distilled fragrances from herbs and flowers with odors such as apple, bergamot, carnation, coconut, jasmine, lavender, lilac, peach, rose, thyme, violet, and dozens more. Use essential oils with caution — they're powerful!

WREATHS

A nice way to enjoy summer is to retreat to a cool place and make an herb wreath. Wreaths capture the fragrance and beauty of herbs, putting them on display where everyone can appreciate them. They also make great gifts for just about any occasion.

Start with a wreath frame. You can use an open wire frame and stuff it with moss or with fresh, sweet-scented herbs such as sweet Annie artemisia or sweet clover. Let the stems wilt before putting them in the frame so you can pack them in firmly. Then leave the stuffed frame in a warm, airy place to dry thoroughly. If you don't have anything handy to stuff a wire frame with, you can wrap the frame with green florist's tape. (Once you cover the frame with herbs you won't see it anyway.) Marty Sickinger of Sunnybrook Farms also uses an "herbary disk," a double set of pegs secured in a round board in a wreath shape. You can fill the space between the sets of pegs with herbal wreath stuffing and wrap it up with florist's wire to make your own wreath.

Or you can buy a straw wreath, grapevine wreath, or a plastic foam wreath for the base. Marty Sickinger suggests that you choose a dense foam that you can peg herbs into without the foam crumbling. To give foam wreath frames a fancier look, cover them with gray Spanish moss and use herbs and flowers here and there for highlights. Or make a woodland wreath by covering a plastic foam base with sheet moss.

Decorate the wreath with fresh or dried herbs such as flowers of basil, oregano, lavender, yarrow, perilla, and thyme; stems of sage, artemisia, rosemary, and thyme; and seed sprays of sorrel. Use finely cut scented geranium leaves, such as 'Fern Leaf' and 'Dr. Livingstone'. For more color, combine herbs with dried everlasting flowers such as amaranth, cockscomb, strawflowers, statice, flowering onions, globe amaranth, sea holly, and love-in-a-mist or dried pods of poppies, teasel, and milkweed. Some people make wreaths that fit a main color scheme, but it's great to experiment. Use culinary herbs, but don't expect them to be used later in cooking. Hanging wreaths collect dust over time.

Develop a color scheme with two primary colors and a contrasting accent color. I like silver foliage and blue flowers with a touch of pink; I also like purple and yellow flowers with a background of green foliage.

Secure the herbs and flowers to the wreath with wire or a hot glue gun (both are available at most craft stores), but use care that you don't burn yourself. Or you can tie the herbs on with green florist's wire.

I prefer the wiring method because it gives me a lot of flexibility. I wire together small bundles of herbs with a few taller sprigs of foliage in the back and a flower or two in the front. For a 12-inch-diameter wreath, the bundles end up about 4 inches long after I trim off the excess at the bottom; they're a couple inches wide at the top (narrower at the base where they are wired together). But you can make them longer or shorter for bigger or smaller wreaths. Then, I put the bundles on the wreath by wrapping their bases with more wire.

I keep the color scheme in mind as I make the herb bundles. I can combine all three colors in each bundle. For example, in the purple and yellow scheme, I might put a green scented geranium leaf in the back of a bundle and in the front use a purple sage sprig and a yellow statice flower spike. Or I might put only one or two colors in each to give the finished wreath an interesting pattern.

To make patterns, mentally divide the wreath into thirds — the inside rim, outside rim, and center of the wreath. You can use one kind of bundle or one main color on the inside and outside and reserve the center for a contrasting color. Or you can use similar colors to zigzag up the wreath, moving them from outside, to center, to inside and back again as you cover progressively more of the wreath.

When you have your game plan worked out, you're ready to apply the bundles. Start by laying three bundles next to each other on the inside, center, and outside of a single location on the frame. Secure them to the wreath by looping green florist's wire over the bundle's wired bases and twisting the loose end around the running strand of wire to knot it in place. Then lay three more bundles over the base of the previous bundles so they cover the wires. Loop the florist's wire around their bases. Continue in this manner until you've covered the entire wreath. Then cut the wire and twist it on to a nearby wire to hold it in place.

Hang your wreath indoors out of the weather. If you want to store it, pack it in a rigid box to keep the delicate dried flowers from getting crushed.

© Kevin Kennefick

© Kevin Kennefick

© Kevin Kennefick

(Top Left) Bundle herb sprigs together and fasten with florist's wire.

(Top Right) Lay the wired sprigs on the frame, overlapping the stems above with each succeeding layer of herbs. Work your way around the circle, covering center and outer edge completely.

(Left) If you work with fresh herbs, lay the wreath flat until the herbs are dry, then hang indoors in a protected area.

A Grower's Guide

There are hundreds of herbs that you can use to brighten up your garden and your life. The only challenge is choosing which ones to grow. Do you want herbs that provide you with garden beauty, fragrance, flavoring, decoration — or all the above? This Grower's Guide will tell you everything you need to grow delightful common and unusual herbs. You will also find references to these herbs scattered throughout the rest of the book. (Check the index to access that information.)

Symbol Key

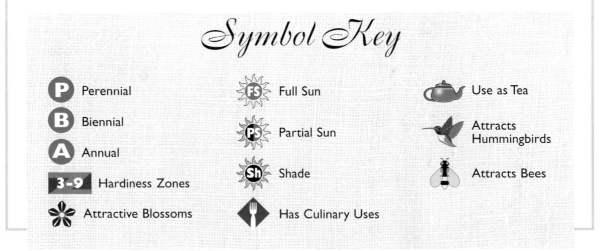

P Perennial

B Biennial

A Annual

3-9 Hardiness Zones

✿ Attractive Blossoms

FS Full Sun

PS Partial Sun

Sh Shade

🍴 Has Culinary Uses

🫖 Use as Tea

🐦 Attracts Hummingbirds

🐝 Attracts Bees

Achillea millefolium – Yarrow

Family: Compositae
Native of Eurasia

Appearance: Aromatic, handsome, finely cut, almost evergreen leaves that range from bright green to grayish. White, pink, or red flowers come in summer and fall on stems that stretch up about 3 feet high. The stems flop easily, especially in rich soil and inadequate sun.

Growing Know-How: Plant in well-drained soil of low fertility. Space 12 to 18 inches apart. Divide every couple of years to extend the otherwise-short life. Once established, yarrow can tolerate drought.

Propagation: You can grow many forms of this yarrow from seed. For the best results with improved cultivars, propagate by division.

Cultivars: You can get excellent floral displays from yarrow cultivars such as 'Cerise Queen' and 'Fire King' and also from hybrids such as 'Appleblossom', 'Fanal', and 'Salmon Beauty'.

Potential Problems: Provide well-drained soil and good air circulation to discourage powdery mildew and root rot.

Harvesting and Using: This old-fashioned medicinal plant is grown primarily for its flowers, which are excellent for fresh or dried arrangements. Dry the flowers in silica gel to preserve the color.

Related Herbs: 'Coronation Gold' *(A. filipendulina)* has broader, fernlike leaves and wide heads of golden flowers that dry beautifully without silica gel.

Sneezewort *(A. ptarmica)* is a vigorous spreader that produces baby's breath–like flowers on sometimes floppy stems.

Woolly yarrow *(A. tomentosa)* is a 12-inch-high edging plant with finely cut gray leaves and golden flowers.

Agastache foeniculum – Anise Hyssop

Family: Labiatae
Native of Southwestern United States

Appearance: Attractive, licorice-scented plant with toothed leaves on square stems and spikes of blue-purple flowers in summer and fall. It reaches about 4 feet tall, forming a vase shape.

Growing Know-How: Grows best in sun but will tolerate a little light shade. Plant in fertile, well-drained soil. Fertilize once or twice during the growing season with a balanced organic fertilizer, or mulch with compost.

Propagation: Grows easily from seed. Start the seed indoors about 6 weeks before the last spring frost. Or, in fall, sow the seed directly where you want plants to grow. You can also move self-sown seedlings.

Potential Problems: If the plant receives too much nitrogen or too little sun, it may need staking.

Harvesting and Using: Pinch off leaves or sprigs any time for making into tea. You can dry the leaves for potpourri. Flowers make a pretty garnish for fruit salads, iced tea, and desserts.

Alchemilla vulgaris – Lady's Mantle

Family: Rosaceae
Native of Northern Europe

Appearance: Has fuzzy, round, scalloped leaves displayed in a low mound about 12 inches tall. It puts out generous sprays of yellow flowers, prolifically in late spring and occasionally through the summer.

Growing Know-How: Plant in moist soil and sun in cool climates or light shade in warm climates. Space plants 18 inches apart. Deadhead after blooming to keep a neat appearance. Irrigate and mulch in dry weather. Fertilize in spring with a balanced organic fertilizer.

Propagation: Lady's mantle is easy to start from divisions in spring or fall as long as you keep the soil moist. It will also grow from seed, but it takes two years to get large enough to flower.

Potential Problems: Keep garden soil from drying out to prevent browning of leaf edges.

Harvesting and Using: Lady's mantle makes a nice edging or middle-of-the-border plant. You can also dry the flowers for potpourri, dried flower arrangements, and wreaths.

Related Herbs: Alpine lady's mantle *(A. alpina)* is a creeping ground cover that grows to 8 inches high.

A. glaucescens is also low growing but has silver-edged leaves.

Yarrow

Anise Hyssop

Lady's Mantle

179

Allium sativum – Garlic

Family: Allium

Native of Siberia

Appearance: Garlic produces flat, bladelike leaves that reach 18 inches high. Some bulbs will also produce a twisting flower stalk that matures into small bulblets. Below ground, individual cloves form in a round bulb that varies slightly in shape, color, and flavor depending on the variety and even on growing conditions.

Growing Know-How: Plant in full sun and loose, well-drained, rich soil. Keep weed-free and fertilize in fall and spring with a balanced organic fertilizer. Water to maintain evenly moist soil, but let the soil dry out just before harvesting. Remove any flower stalks that may arise. If you plant a few smaller cloves deeper and closer than the recommended spacing below, you can harvest the tasty greens instead of the bulbs.

Propagation: Plant individual cloves 1 to 2 inches deep and 4 inches apart in late fall in warm climates or early fall in cool climates. In warm climates, you can get better results by prechilling the bulbs in the refrigerator for several months before planting. Mulch with straw over winter.

Cultivars: There are quite a few cultivars of garlic available in mail-order seed and herb catalogues, so don't limit yourself to growing what you find in the grocery store. Check catalogues to get an idea of availability and ask what cultivars grow best in your area.

Ron Engleman of Filaree Farm (a garlic nursery in Okanogan, Washington) explains that the best flavored garlic is the Rocombole type such as 'Spanish Roja' or 'German Red', which have rich, full flavor without much heat. But Rocombole garlics also have a flower stalk that you need to cut out, so they take a little more work to grow. Hard-necked porcelain types such as 'Romanian Red' have clean white bulbs. Purple-stripe types include cultivars such as 'Red Czar'. You can also grow soft-necked garlics such as easy-growing artichoke garlics 'Inchelium Red' or silver-skinned California commercial garlics such as 'Silverwhite', which do best in areas with mild winters.

Potential Problems: Provide well-drained soil to prevent bulb rot and other diseases.

Harvesting and Using: Dig up bulbs when the foliage begins to yellow in late summer. Cure in a warm, airy location for 2 weeks and then move to a cold (35°–50°F), airy location for winter storage. You can braid nonflowering types after the foliage dries slightly. Garlic can even be frozen whole and mashed into your favorite recipe.

Roast garlic cloves whole for a milder flavor or chop them finely for maximum flavor. Add to any meats, salads, vinegars, breads, and more. You can make pesto out of the cloves and leaves.

Related Herbs: Giant garlic (*A. scorodoprasum*) is a half-hardy perennial from Europe. It sends up a tall, curling stem with flowers that develop into small bulbs. The foliage dies back after the flowers fade, allowing the bulbs to fall to the ground where they'll sprout. Harvest the little bulbs and the leaves, which have a mild garlic flavor.

Elephant garlic (*A. ampeloprasum*) is actually a leek that produces huge bulbs and cloves that are mildly garlic flavored.

Allium schoenoprasum – Chives

Family: Allium

Native of Eurasia

Appearance: These hearty growers form tubular leaves up to 24 inches high. In late spring they have lavender, ball-shaped heads of flowers. Both the flowers and the foliage are edible.

Growing Know-How: Give chives full sun and well-drained soil of average fertility. Space plants about 18 inches apart. When the flowers begin to fade, cut them all off at the base of the plant if you want to prevent them from self-sowing. Some flowers may appear sporadically through the summer, so keep your eye out for them — they make excellent cut flowers. In late summer, you can dig up a plant or two and put them in large pots to keep in a cool windowsill or light garden for winter harvests. Leave the pots outdoors until after a few frosts for best indoor leaf production.

Propagation: Chives are easy to start from seed. Start seeds indoors 6 weeks before the last spring frost. Set them out when the weather is mild. Or transplant a self-sown seedling that's emerged in your garden, or divide a mature plant. Renew older plants by dividing every 5 years or so.

Cultivars: 'Ruby Gem' has gray foliage and red flowers.

Potential Problems: Plant in well-drained soil to prevent root rot.

Harvesting and Using: When you harvest the leaves or flowers, cut them off at the base to keep it looking tidy. Use the fresh foliage with eggs, cream cheese, salads, soups, butters, and burgers. You can chop up extra leaves by hand or puree them with a little oil to make a pesto to freeze. Use the flowers to garnish salads or soups, and to make lavender-colored vinegar. Be sure to wash the flowers out well, though, because they may harbor insects.

Related Herbs: Garlic or oriental chives (*A. tuberosum*) have a pleasant garlic flavor long used in oriental cooking. They have flat leaves that reach a foot high and edible, fragrant, white flowers during the summer. They spread reasonably slowly on rhizomes but can be more aggressive about self-sowing. Harvest as you would regular chives. Propagate by division or transplant self-sown seedlings.

Garlic

Garlic Chives

Chives

181

Aloysia triphylla – Lemon Verbena

Family: Verbenaceae
Native of South America

Appearance: Lemon-scented tender shrub grows up to 10 feet high. Whorls of leaves along branches and small, white or violet flowers.

Growing Know-How: Plant in full sun in cool climates or light shade in warm climates and loose, well-drained but rich soil. Can be grown in a pot. Fertilize once a month.

In cool climates, bring it in to a cool, bright location indoors. If leaves drop, keep soil on the dry side until they begin to grow again.

Propagation: Take cuttings of firm shoots in summer.

Potential Problems: Whiteflies, aphids, and spider mites.

Harvesting and Using: Use leaves fresh or dried in teas, or add them to dressings, fruit salads, and drinks. Remove stiff leaves before serving.

Anethum graveolens – Dill

Family: Umbelliferae
Native of Europe/Mediterranean region

Appearance: Quick-growing herb with fine, ferny leaves on hollow, upright stems up to 3 feet high. Umbrella-like heads of yellow flowers are great for seasoning or fresh-cut flowers.

Growing Know-How: Plant in full sun and well-drained soil. Space plants 12 inches apart. Plant succession crops in warm climates. Fertilize when plants start flowering with a sprinkling of fertilizer high in potassium and phosphorus.

Propagation: Sow outdoors in fall or spring.

Cultivars: For compact cultivars, try 'Bouquet' and 'Fernleaf'; for slow-bolting cultivars, try 'Tetra' and 'Dukat'.

Potential Problems: Parsley worms, the striped caterpillars that become black swallowtail butterflies, love dill. Transfer them gently to a wild Queen Anne's lace plant.

Harvesting and Using: Harvest the leaves or cut the entire plant back once it gets to be about 12 inches tall. Harvest seed when it begins to turn brown. Hang seed heads in a warm, airy location over a catch cloth. Use fresh, dried, or frozen leaves on fish, in creamy spreads, with eggs, potato salad, or butter. Use seeds with vegetables, soups, meats, pickles, and breads.

Angelica archangelica – Angelica

Family: Umbelliferae
Native of Northern Europe

Appearance: Large plant with broad, toothed leaves. In its second year, a spectacular flower stem emerges and grows 6 feet high into a broad, umbrella-shaped cluster of white flowers.

Growing Know-How: Grow in moist, rich soil in light shade, or full sun in cool climates. Mulch and irrigate if the weather gets hot and dry. Fertilize in spring and midsummer. To keep your original plant growing for another year, cut off the flower stalk. If it goes to seed, the plant will die but may self-seed.

Propagation: Let some seeds self-sow. Commercial seed may need pretreatment to germinate. Sprinkle seed on moist growing mix and leave the pots outdoors from fall to spring; cold helps them germinate better. Or put the seed in moist growing mix in the refrigerator for 6 weeks. Then move to a warm, bright spot. Plant seedlings in the garden when they're small to minimize root disturbance.

Potential Problems: Blast aphids with the garden hose or spray with insecticidal soap. In warm climates, discourage rot by planting in well-drained soil and light shade. Can't take hot summers.

Harvesting and Using: Cut young licorice-flavored flower stems to slice and candy or use with rhubarb in pie. Use angelica leaves and small sprigs in salads.

Related Herbs: Korean angelica *(A. gigas)* has red stems and flower buds, purplish foliage, and white flowers. A wild species, *A. atropurpurea,* is common in parts of the northeastern United States. It should never be eaten because it is easy to confuse its reddish stems with some very toxic plants.

Anthriscus cereifolium – Chervil

Family: Umbelliferae
Native of Eurasia

Appearance: Resembles parsley with light green leaves and umbrella-like clusters of white flowers on stems up to 2 feet high. You can find both curly and flat leaf forms.

Growing Know-How: Thrives in cool, mild weather — bolts in the heat. Space plants 6 to 12 inches apart in moist, fertile soil and light shade. Fertilize in early and midsummer with fish emulsion. Grow indoors in the winter.

Propagation: Sow seeds shallowly in early spring or summer for a fall crop. Plants may bolt if you try to move them.

Harvesting and Using: Use fresh leaves as you would parsley. Freeze leaves to preserve mild flavor; dried chervil has little flavor.

Chervil

Angelica

Lemon Verbena

Dill

183

Armoracia rusticana – Horseradish

Family: Cruciferae

Native of Europe

Appearance: Rugged-looking leaves up to 3 feet long that emerge from the ground in a clump. Sometimes plants produce white flowers. Below ground, the roots grow deep and aggressively.

Growing Know-How: In fall or early spring, work soil 2 feet down and plant horseradish in full sun and moist, rich, well-drained soil 6 to 18 inches apart.

Propagation: Easy to grow from 6- to 8-inch pieces of root.

Potential Problems: Remove roots in fall to prevent spread.

Harvesting and Using: Dig roots in fall or spring. Peel and grind in a blender or food processor with vinegar and salt to make horseradish sauce. Watch out, the fumes will be strong! Store in a sterilized canning jar in the refrigerator. Or keep a few roots in a bucket of sand in a damp root cellar.

Artemisia absinthium - Wormwood

Family: Compositae

Native of Eurasia

Appearance: Grows about 3 feet tall and has fragrant, divided, silver leaves and small green flowers during the summer.

Growing Know-How: Grow in well-drained soil and full sun. If necessary, it will tolerate light shade.

Propagation: Take cuttings in spring or sow seed in spring or fall. Space 3 feet apart. Divide as needed.

Potential Problems: May need staking if grown without sufficient sun. Can self-sow and get weedy if not deadheaded. If foliage discolors after flowering, cut entire plant back to resprout. It is subject to fungus in hot humid weather, as are all artemisias.

Harvesting and Using: Used to repel moths and as garden accent.

Related Herbs: 'Silver King' artemisia (*A. ludoviciana*) has silver foliage and handsome silver flower buds that dry easily and are great in wreaths and arrangements. Prefers sun and well-drained, sandy soil. Spreads quickly enough to be considered weedy.

'Silver Mound' artemesia (*A. schmidtiana*) forms a low mound of finely cut silver leaves. Great for edging an herb garden. Needs well-drained soil of limited fertility and full sun.

Unlike the previous artemisias, perennial mugwort (*A. vulgaris*) has finely cut green leaves and large yellow panicles of flowers in late summer. Can reach 6 feet high. Give it full sun and well-drained soil. Start seeds indoors in early spring and transplant out after the last spring frost. Once established, it will spread generously. Remove flowers; it self-sows easily.

Southernwood (*A. abrotanum*) has finely cut, green leaves but it only reaches about 3 feet high. It has a wonderfully strong, almost citrusy aroma used in moth-repellent sachets. Start from cuttings or divisions.

Sweet Annie (*A. annua*) is an annual that gets to be 10 feet tall with finely divided green leaves, a lovely apple scent, and small yellow flowers. Great for stuffing herb wreaths. Simple to start from seeds and can self-sow prolifically.

A. dracunculus var. sativa – French Tarragon

Family: Compositae

Native of Eurasia

Appearance: A 2- to 3-foot bush with narrow leaves and a bold anise flavor and fragrance. Seldom flowers and never produces seed.

Growing Know-How: Plant in well-drained but moderately fertile soil and full sun. Space plants 18 inches apart.

Propagation: If you already have tarragon, you can divide it to make more plants. You can also take cuttings in summer.

Potential Problems: Divide every couple of years; replant healthiest section. French tarragon cannot form seed.

Harvesting and Using: Harvest sprigs through the summer but stop harvesting in fall to discourage winter damage. Use the leaves fresh, dried, or frozen with chicken, fish or cheese dishes, cream sauces, herbal vinegars, and herbal mustards.

Related Herbs: Russian tarragon (*A. dracunculus*) resembles French tarragon but with much inferior flavor. It is grown from seed and gets to be 5 feet tall. Russian tarragon can form seed.

Borago officinalis – Borage

Family: Boraginaceae

Native of Europe

Appearance: Long, fuzzy leaves and flopping stems up to about 2 feet high. It produces many star-shaped blue or purple flowers.

Growing Know-How: Grow in light, dry soil and full sun, although it will tolerate light shade. Unless you pinch the plant back frequently, you may need to stake it to keep it upright. Borage is short-lived; sow successive crops.

Propagation: Sow the seed in spring and summer.

Potential Problems: Mulch to prevent rotting of lower leaves. Pick off and destroy Japanese beetles.

Harvesting and Using: If you don't mind the prickly texture, you can eat the tender young leaves. The cucumber-flavored flowers are excellent for garnishes or vinegars; you can also dry them.

Horseradish

Wormwood

French Tarragon

Borage

Brassica hirta – White Mustard

Family: Cruciferae
Native of Mediterranean region

Appearance: Handsome when it starts to flower. Toothed leaves on tall, skinny plants up to 4 feet high. Attractive flowers are a perky shade of yellow.

Growing Know-How: Grow during cool weather in fertile, moist soil and full sun. Water if necessary to keep the soil moist. You can also grow in a container in a brightly lit, cool area indoors.

Propagation: Direct sow seed. It comes up quickly.

Potential Problems: Deadhead to minimize self-sowing.

Harvesting and Using: You can eat the spicy-flavored young leaves in salads and stir-fries. Collect the seed when mature but before the fruit splits open. Dry to store them. Grind them with vinegar or wine, or toast them in oil.

Related Herbs: Black mustard *(B. nigra)* can grow to 6 feet tall and has smaller but more strongly flavored seeds.

Brown mustard *(B. juncea)* is grown for its foliage, which can be ruby-colored or ruffled, and also for its seeds.

Calendula officinalis – Pot Marigold

Family: Compositae
Native of Europe

Appearance: Produces single or double flowers in shades of yellow, orange, and gold. Can grow up to 18 inches high.

Growing Know-How: Thrives in mild, cool weather, full sun or light shade, and well-drained, moderately fertile soil. Plant about 12 inches apart. To help a spring-blooming plant rebloom in fall, cut it back by one-third and fertilize in summer. Will flower in a bright window or light garden during winter, but the plant can get straggly indoors. Remove fading flowers to encourage additional bloom.

Propagation: Sow outdoors in spring, late summer, or (in mild climates) fall. Or start the seedlings indoors 6 weeks before the last spring frost. You can also transplant self-sown seedlings.

Cultivars: 'Bon Bon' is a series of apricot, yellow, or orange flowers that reach only 12 inches high and are extra early blooming. 'Prince' is a series of golden, orange, or orange with red flowers on stems up to 3 feet high, perfect for cutting.

Potential Problems: Keep in well-drained soil in a site with good air circulation to prevent fungal diseases. Watch for aphids, especially after dry spells; wash aphids off with a strong spray from a hose.

Harvesting and Using: Use flowers as a garnish or component of salads. They give a golden color and unique flavor to soups, breads, and vinegars.

Capsicum annuum – Chile Peppers

Family: Solanaceae
Native of South/Central America

Appearance: Glossy leaves with pointed tips and moderately attractive white flowers on plants about 30 inches high.

Growing Know-How: Plant after the last spring frost in fertile, moist, but well-drained soil and full sun. Space 12 to 18 inches apart. Fertilize monthly with a fertilizer higher in nitrogen in early summer and a fertilizer higher in potassium and phosphorus after flowering. For the hottest flavor, let the peppers ripen fully in hot, sunny weather.

Propagation: Start seed indoors 8 to 10 weeks before last spring frost. Keep seedlings at 75°F to encourage faster germination.

Cultivars: Try very hot, slender 'Cayenne' peppers to make dried pepper flakes. Short, stubby 'Jalapeno' peppers have a slow burn and are great pickled. 'Anaheim' chile peppers are flavorful and milder — excellent roasted and skinned.

Harvesting and Using: Harvest in green or ripe stage. Dry thin-fleshed peppers such as cayenne and sprinkle the flakes on food. Roast thick-fleshed peppers and use as a spicy vegetable.

Related Herbs: Habanero peppers *(C. chinense)* have super-hot, cube-shaped orange peppers.

Carum carvi – Caraway

Family: Umbelliferae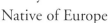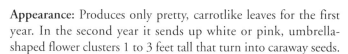
Native of Europe

Appearance: Produces only pretty, carrotlike leaves for the first year. In the second year it sends up white or pink, umbrella-shaped flower clusters 1 to 3 feet tall that turn into caraway seeds.

Growing Know-How: Give well-drained soil of moderate fertility, full sun, and freedom from excessive heat and humidity. Space plants about 8 inches apart. Fertilize when the plants flower with a balanced organic fertilizer. (Caraway is hardy to zones 8 to 10 if the summers are not too hot.)

Propagation: Sow outdoors in fall or early spring. Or start the seed indoors in a peat pot 4 weeks before the last spring frost. Move the pot into the garden when plants are still small, and remove the bottom of the peat pot gently so you won't damage the taproot.

Potential Problems: Harvest seeds to prevent rampant self-sowing.

Harvesting and Using: Harvest the seed in late summer when it is ripe. Hang the seed heads over newspaper and let them dry for several days in a warm, airy location. Collect the seed and freeze for 48 hours to kill any possible pests. Store in an airtight jar in a cool, dark location. Use in goulash, soups, cabbage, breads, applesauce, or cottage cheese dishes.

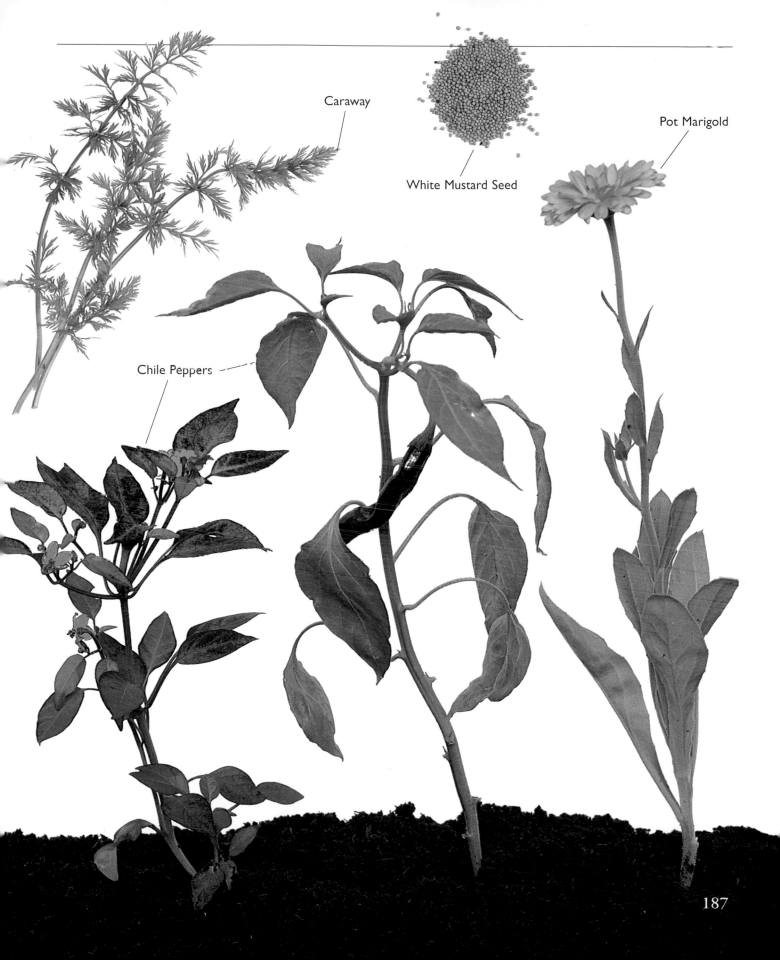

Caraway

White Mustard Seed

Pot Marigold

Chile Peppers

187

Coriandrum sativum – Cilantro/Coriander

Family: Umbelliferae

Native of Mediterranean region

Appearance: The foliage (called "cilantro") looks like parsley but has an exceptional sweet-musky flavor. Produces pale pink flowers during the summer; these ripen into the sweetly aromatic coriander seed. The plant, in flower, can reach 3 feet high.

Growing Know-How: Plant during mild weather in moist, rich soil and full sun. Benefits from light shade in warmer weather. Space plants 4 inches apart. If you want to harvest the leaves, fertilize a week after planting with fish emulsion to provide extra nitrogen. Use a balanced organic fertilizer when you want to harvest for seed.

Propagation: Sow seed outdoors in early spring. If you want a regular supply of cilantro, sow every two weeks through the summer, as plants bolt fairly quickly.

Cultivars: For leaves, plant slower-bolting cultivars.

Potential Problems: Eliminate pests in harvested seeds by freezing the seeds for 48 hours once they are dried.

Harvesting and Using: Harvest leaves of young plants before they bolt to use in Mexican, Caribbean, and oriental dishes. Collect seed when it begins to turn brown in summer. Dry in a warm, airy place over a cloth or hang upside-down to dry inside a paper bag. Rub a handful of seeds between your hands to release the edible seed from the seed coat. Freeze seeds for 48 hours before storing in an airtight jar in a cool, dark place. Use ground seeds in baked goods, soups, casseroles, or potpourri.

Crocus sativus – Saffron Crocus

Family: Iridaceae

Native of Eurasia

Appearance: Has lavender flowers, blooms in fall, and bears fragrant stigma tips that are dried to make the spice saffron. Flowers reach 5 inches high and the narrow, bladelike leaves 12 inches high.

Growing Know-How: In early fall, plant in full sun and fertile but well-drained soil. Space bulbs 3 inches apart in large masses for the best ornamental display. Mark their position on a garden plan or with golf tees, so you don't disturb them when they are dormant.

Propagation: Corms divide easily after foliage has died back.

Cultivars: You can find white-flowered forms.

Potential Problems: Be certain you buy saffron crocus and not autumn crocus (*Colchicum* spp.), which has larger, showier flowers and is poisonous. Provide well-drained soil to avoid rot.

Harvesting and Using: Pluck off the brightly colored tips — the stigmas — inside the flowers and dry to store. They're tiny, so you'll need a lot of flowers to get a small harvest. Use them in rice and noodle dishes.

Eruca vesicaria subsp. sativa – Arugula/Roquette

Family: Cruciferae

Native of Mediterranean region

Appearance: This low-growing, garlic-mustard-flavored herb has notched, oblong leaves 4 to 10 inches long. It will bolt to produce white flowers and seed a month or two after planting.

Growing Know-How: Plant during cool but mild weather in moist, fertile soil. Plant it in wide rows or use it as a temporary edging. Fertilize with fish emulsion every 3 weeks, especially if the seedlings aren't growing quickly enough. You can also grow arugula during winter in a cold frame or indoor light garden.

Propagation: Sow seed outdoors in early through late spring and in late summer and fall. Young seedlings may survive winter.

Potential Problems: Flea beetles can gnaw small holes in the foliage. Cover with floating row covers to keep them away.

Harvesting and Using: Pick the foliage when young and tender. Use it in salads and stir-fries.

Arugula

Saffron Crocus corms

Coriander

189

Foeniculum vulgare – Fennel

Family: Umbelliferae
Native of Europe

Appearance: Common fennel looks much like a tall version of dill, only the stems are solid and the aroma resembles licorice. In summer, the plant sends up 4-foot-high clusters of yellow, umbrella-shaped flowers. The seed matures in late summer.

Growing Know-How: Plant in full sun and well-drained soil of average fertility. Space 12 inches apart.

Propagation: Direct-sow seed in spring. May self-sow.

Cultivars: Florence fennel, grown as a cool-season annual, has unusual succulent, licorice-flavored stem bases that are good in salads, stir-fries, and sautees. The plant reaches only 18 inches high. Provide rich soil and full sun. Sow the seed outdoors in spring for summer harvest or summer for fall harvest. For extra-tender stem bases, mound soil up around the base to blanch them.

Bronze fennel has handsome dark foliage that provides contrasting color in the garden and as a garnish on a dinner plate.

Potential Problems: Knock aphids off with a strong spray from the garden hose or treat them with insecticidal soap. Black swallowtail butterfly caterpillars are attracted to fennel and to dill, parsley, chervil, and many other herbs in the Umbelliferae Family. Let them have their share so you can enjoy the beauty of the butterflies, or transfer them gently to a wild Queen Anne's lace plant.

Harvesting and Using: Harvest seeds of common fennel before they turn totally brown and self-sow. Dry the seeds as you would dill and use them in baked goods, soups, and sausages. Use the leaves to season fish, carrots, and other vegetables.

Galium odoratum – Sweet Woodruff

Family: Rubiaceae
Native of Europe

Appearance: Handsome ground cover with whorls of rich green leaves and a lacy blanket of white flowers in spring. Grows about 6 inches high.

Growing Know-How: A great herb for shaded gardens with rich, moist soil. Space plants 18 to 24 inches apart. Mulch in spring as the plant emerges, and keep the soil evenly moist.

Propagation: Can easily be propagated by division.

Potential Problems: Avoid full sun and dry soil, which can cause foliage to yellow and wilt. It goes dormant in hot summers.

Harvesting and Using: Pick sprigs just before flowering for the best fragrance. Dry the sprigs in a cool, airy place for fragrance. Use dried leaves in potpourri.

Hyssopus officinalis – Hyssop

Family: Labiatae
Native of Europe

Appearance: Has thin, dark green leaves that are handsome when clipped into a knot or edging. If you don't clip the plant, the foliage can reach up to 2 feet high and produce handsome, long-blooming blue, white, or pink flowers that stretch up even higher.

Growing Know-How: Plant in well-drained soil in sun or light shade. Space 12 inches apart. Cut plants back and fertilize with a balanced organic fertilizer in spring to encourage fresh new growth.

Cultivars: 'Aristata' is a dwarf hyssop that needs tighter spacing to grow into a mass or edging.

Propagation: Start hyssop from seed in fall or spring or from cuttings and divisions. You can also transplant self-sown seedlings.

Potential Problems: Grow in well-drained soil to prevent disease problems.

Harvesting and Using: Hyssop is a fragrant ornamental, good for clipping into a knot or edging or leaving unclipped for cut flowers.

Laurus nobilis – Sweet Bay

Family: Lauraceae
Native of Mediterranean region

Appearance: An evergreen tree with dark, glossy, oval leaves. Can reach 60 feet high in native lands but seldom reaches 6 feet high when grown in a pot in cooler climates.

Growing Know-How: Grow outdoors in fertile, well-drained soil or in a pot with compost-enriched growing mix. Give the tree full sun or light shade and keep it out of blustery winds. If you bring it indoors in winter, put it in a cool, brightly lit location. Healthy trees respond well to pruning and shearing.

Propagation: Buy your tree from a nursery. Once it's growing you can try taking cuttings, but they take many months to root.

Potential Problems: If your bay tree gets scale, scrub them off with rubbing alcohol.

Harvesting and Using: Harvest leaves to use whole in meat dishes, stews, and soups; the flavor stands up to a lot of cooking. But be sure to pull the leaves out before serving so no one chokes on them. You can also dry and pulverize bay leaves to use as a powder in cooking. Or use whole leaves in potpourri and herbal wreaths.

Sweet Bay

Sweet Woodruff

Fennel

Hyssop

191

Lavandula angustifolia – English Lavender

Family: Labiatae

Native of Mediterranean region

Appearance: Evergreen shrub with narrow, silver, needlelike leaves on bushy plant up to 18 inches tall. The lavender-blue flowers appear in summer and stretch up about 6 inches higher.

Growing Know-How: Plant in full sun and clean, well-drained soil 12 inches apart. Mulch with an inch or two of coarse sand. Give the plant time to reemerge in spring before trimming. In areas with mild winters, you can shear growing lavender into a low hedge, knot, or edging. Remove faded flowers.

Propagation: Most lavender seed germinates slowly and erratically. Propagate most cultivars from cuttings, layering, or division.

Cultivars: Dozens of cultivars are available. 'Lavender Lady', which reaches about 10 inches high, grows relatively quickly from seed. It can flower the first year after planting if started indoors in late winter, so it can be grown as an annual in climates too cold for other lavenders.

'Munstead' forms a neat mound 12 inches high. It is one of the hardiest cultivars. 'Jean Davis' reaches only 12 inches high and has pink flowers. 'Twickel Purple' has purple flowers on a 2-foot-high plant.

Potential Problems: Plant in very well-drained soil to prevent rot. Encourage good air circulation to prevent foliage diseases.

Harvesting and Using: Lavender is an attractive ornamental with a wonderful fragrance. Harvest flower stalks when in bud; bunch and dangle them to dry in a warm, airy location. Use flowers in potpourri, sachets, wreaths, flower arrangements, and cooking.

Related Herbs: There are a number of species that are not hardy in northern areas. Where winters are cold, you can grow these species as annuals or bring them indoors during winter. They are listed here by botanical names.

L. dentata, a native of Spain and southern France, has toothed, green leaves on stems that can reach up to 3 feet high. The flowers can be blue or white. 'Candicans' is a cultivar with gray leaves. 'Linda Ligon' has white-spotted leaves. *L. stoechas* reaches up to 2 feet high with extra-early, dark purple flowers. Woolly lavender *(L. lanata)* has woolly white leaves and purple flowers. It gets to be 2 feet high.

Levisticum officinale – Lovage

Family: Umbelliferae

Native of Southern Europe

Appearance: Leathery, celery-like basal leaves and a tall flower stalk that grows 6 feet high. The yellow umbels of flowers emerge in summer and can be quite showy. When they fade, the foliage can yellow.

Growing Know-How: Plant in moist, fertile soil and full sun (or light shade in warmer climates). Fertilize with balanced organic fertilizer in spring and mulch in summer. Remove young flower stalks to keep foliage fresh longer.

Propagation: Start seed indoors 6 weeks before last spring frost or sow seed outdoors in fall for spring germination.

Potential Problems: Remove leaves with brown leaf miners' tunnels.

Harvesting and Using: Use fresh or dried leaves with salads, potatoes, stews, or any dish that calls for low salt, fresh celery, or dried celery leaves. (Lovage has a much stronger flavor than celery, so use with restraint.) You can also freeze pureed leaves and add them to sauces and soups. Use the dried seeds as you would celery seed and the fresh or dried roots in teas or long-cooking soups.

Matricaria recutita – German Chamomile

Family: Compositae

Native of Northern Europe

Appearance: Fine, ferny leaves and daisylike flowers on stems about 24 inches high. Apple-scented flowers can be used in tea. The plants fade quickly after flowering.

Growing Know-How: Plant in full sun and well-drained soil of average fertility. Replant in midsummer for second harvest.

Propagation: Sow annual chamomile in early spring and again in summer for a succession of harvests. It may self-sow once started.

Harvesting and Using: Harvest flowers to use fresh or dried in teas. If you're allergic to ragweed, may cause an allergic reaction. Use chamomile in potpourri. Flowers are used to highlight blonde hair.

Related Herbs: English or Roman chamomile *(Anthemis nobilis)* has a more pungent aroma and is grown primarily as a scented ground cover. Also available as double-flowered 'Flore Plena' or flower-free 'Treneague'.

Melissa officinalis – Lemon Balm

Family: Labiatae

Native of Southern Europe

Appearance: Has intensely lemon-scented, heart-shaped leaves on stems up to 2½ feet high. It produces inconspicuous white flowers in summer and fall. Unlike other mints, it does not produce rapidly spreading runners.

English Lavender

German Chamomile

Lovage

Lemon Balm

193

Growing Know-How: Easy to grow in well-drained, average to sandy soil and full sun to light shade. If growth is slow, fertilize once or twice during the growing season. Deadhead to prevent self-sowing and keep foliage from yellowing.

Propagation: The most convenient way to start lemon balm is by dividing existing plants in spring and fall or transplanting self-sown seedlings in late spring. You can also sow seed outdoors in early spring or start seedlings indoors 8 weeks before the last spring frost. To bring lemon balm indoors for winter, take stem cuttings in midsummer.

Cultivars: You can find variegated lemon balm; give it partial shade to retain leaf color in summer.

Potential Problems: Thin out thickly growing clumps to prevent powdery mildew.

Harvesting and Using: Fresh lemon balm will perfume a room with its lemony scent. But it has more fragrance than flavor and is strongest when fresh. Cut sprigs as you need them through the growing season and use them for herb tea, garnishing iced tea or wine, cooking with poultry or fish, or flavoring soups.

Mentha spp. – Mint

Family: Labiatae
Native of Europe

Appearance: Mints have a square stem and opposite leaves. The stems can reach 2 to 3 feet high and produce small flowers in late summer.

Growing Know-How: Plant mint in moist, fertile soil in light shade. Space plants 3 feet apart and divide often to prevent aggressive spreading. You can also plant mints in sunken containers to slow down their spread. Water to keep the soil evenly moist and fertilize lightly to encourage maximum flavor. Note that species of mint interbreed easily, forming many hybrids that blur distinctions between species.

Propagation: Can be grown from root divisions or stem cuttings.

Potential Problems: Keep manure away from mint to discourage rust disease. Remove any yellow-streaked sprigs to prevent the spread of virus. Treat most insect pests with insecticidal soap.

Harvesting and Using: Harvest sprigs just before flowering or as needed. Use the foliage fresh, frozen, or dried in teas, candied treats, or as flavoring for peas, lamb, potatoes, and other foods.

Related Herbs: Many species and hybrids are available. Some have citrus, ginger, and other mint-blend aromas.

Peppermint (*M.* x *piperita*)

Peppermint is unique in its characteristic peppermint odor. Flowers are small and purple, appearing in late summer. Try the cultivar 'Mitcham' for strong flavor and dark purple stems.

Spearmint (*M. spicata*)

Spearmint has the bold spearmint flavor on a rapidly spreading plant that can reach 3 feet high. The 'Himalayan Silver' cultivar is particularly ornamental.

Curly mint (*M. spicata* 'Crispata')

Curly mint has curly or crinkled, deep green leaves that have subtle spearmint flavor.

Apple mint (*M. suaveolens*)

Apple mint has sweet-smelling leaves that are usually round and hairy. The flowers are white to pale purple. It can tolerate drier sites than many other mints. Use the leaves for fresh flower arrangements or dry them for potpourri.

Pineapple mint (*M. spicata* 'Variegata')

Pineapple mint has variegated leaves that have a mild apple mint flavor. It grows to about 16 inches and complements flowering herbs, such as white-flowering garlic chives.

Corsican mint (*M. requienii*)

Corsican mint is a tiny, creeping plant that only reaches an inch high. Use it between rocks in a moist, shady walk.

English pennyroyal (*M. pulegium*)

English pennyroyal is an old-fashioned medicinal plant. It's used primarily as an insect repellent today. It will tolerate full sun if given evenly moist soil, and it makes an interesting fragrant ground cover or lawn plant.

Peppermint

Curly Mint

Pineapple Mint

English Pennyroyal

Spearmint

Monarda didyma – Bee Balm/Bergamot/ Oswego Tea

Family: Labiatae
Native of North America

Appearance: Has scented, oval leaves with pointed tips on stems up to 3 feet high. It grows in large clumps, spreading continually on runners to colonize more ground. The species has red flowers; selected cultivars and hybrids are white, pink, or purple. The flowers emerge in shaggy clumps during summer; all attract hummingbirds.

Growing Know-How: Give rich, moist but well-drained soil in full sun or light shade. For faster growth, fertilize in spring. Divide every 3 years to keep tidy. If the old central growth dies back, dig up that portion and replace it with fresh soil so new shoots can fill in. Remove faded flowers to encourage additional bloom.

Propagation: Propagate by division or cuttings, or grow the species by seed. Start seedlings indoors 8 to 10 weeks before the last spring frost.

Cultivars: 'Gardenview Scarlet' is somewhat resistant to powdery mildew. 'Marshall's Delight' is mildew-resistant and rose-pink. 'Violet Queen' is lavender-blue and also mildew-resistant.

Potential Problems: The species and many of its cultivars are susceptible to powdery mildew. Use mildew-resistant cultivars, or thin clumps to promote good air circulation. Cut diseased plants back to resprout healthy foliage.

Harvesting and Using: Pick leaves and flowers to add fragrance and color to teas, or dry for potpourri. Use fresh flowers in arrangements or as an edible garnish.

Related Herbs: Wild monarda (*M. fistulosa*) is a perennial with white to lavender flowers. It's a sturdy plant that can hold its own in meadows. A rose-scented, purple-flowered hybrid of this is *M. × media* or *M. fistulosa × tetraploid* (excellent to use in potpourri).

   Lemon mint (*M. citriodora*) is an annual or biennial with white to pink flowers and a lemon scent. It grows up to 2 feet high and is used in tea or potpourri.

Myrrhis odorata – Sweet Cicely

Family: Umbelliferae
Native of Europe

Appearance: Finely cut leaves give it a fernlike look. Reaches 36 inches high with umbrella-shaped clusters of white flowers late spring/early summer. The flowers develop into flavorful seeds.

Growing Know-How: Sweet cicely is a great herb to grow in a lightly shaded garden with loose, rich soil, with lots of organic matter. Space about 18 inches apart. Start with a small plant from a nursery — purchased seeds often don't germinate well.

Propagation: Sweet cicely can be slow to germinate and difficult to transplant, so sow it directly in the site you want, using freshly ripened seeds in the fall. Once it is established, it will often self-sow.

Potential Problems: Deadhead carefully to avoid excessive self-sowing. If aphids attack, blast them off the plant with your garden hose or spray with insecticidal soap.

Harvesting and Using: Sweet cicely seeds have a pleasant flavor that is great in tea or dessert breads. The flavor is strongest in fresh green, unripe seeds. You can also eat the leaves in salads.

Nepeta mussinii – Catmint

Family: Labiatae
Native of Middle East

Appearance: Catmint has opposite gray leaves and handsome, long-blooming spikes of purple or blue flowers on stems up to 15 inches high. Plants often sprawl, so they may seem shorter.

Growing Know-How: Plant catmint in well-drained soil of moderate fertility in full sun or light shade. It blooms prolifically during the summer if you keep it deadheaded.

Propagation: Sow seed outdoors in spring or late summer, or start seedlings indoors 6 weeks before the last frost date. You can also divide existing plants and transplant self-sown seedlings.

Cultivars: The *Nepeta × faassenii* hybrid grows more upright and is sterile. You can only propagate it by cuttings and division. 'Dropmore' has large lavender-blue flowers; 'Snowflake' has white flowers.

Potential Problems: None serious.

Harvesting and Using: The foliage is aromatic but not as appealing to cats as catnip. Catmint's main value is as a long-blooming ornamental, but you can dry the foliage and flowers for potpourri.

Related Herbs: Catnip (*N. cataria*) is a favorite of felines all over the world. It is not as attractive as catmint, producing small white flowers and often getting shaggy close to the end of the growing season. It self-sows with abandon unless deadheaded, but sometimes dies after only a year or two of life. You can harvest the leaves and sprigs for your cats or for tea.

Bee Balm

Sweet Cicely

Catnip

Catmint

Sweet Cicely

197

Ocimum basilicum – Basil

Family: Labiatae   A ✹/✹ ⚒

Native of Pacific Islands

Appearance: Basil grows into a bushy plant 6 inches to several feet high. It has opposite, oval leaves with pointed tips and spikes of small white or pink flowers.

Growing Know-How: For best results, plant basil outdoors in a sunny site, but it will tolerate light shade. Give it moist but well-drained, fertile soil. Fertilize with a water-soluble, organic fertilizer each time you harvest. Pinch off the growing tips to make the plant bushier; remove all flower spikes to prolong harvest. The plants will die with the first fall frost unless you bring them indoors.

Propagation: Grow basil from seed or cuttings. For a head start on the growing season, start seedlings indoors 4 to 6 weeks before the last spring frost.

Varieties and Cultivars: Many cultivars of basil are now readily available. Below are several of the most popular ones.

Sweet basil

Sweet basil varieties have glossy leaves and full basil flavor. One excellent cultivar is 'Genovese'.

Lettuce-leaf basil (*O. b.* var. *crispum*)

Lettuce-leaf basil has extra-broad leaves. Cultivars include 'Mammoth', slow-bolting 'Napoletano', and much-ruffled 'Green Ruffles'.

Bush basils

Bush basils, which make good edgings, range from 3 to 12 inches high. They include 'Spicy Globe', 'Bush', 'Tiny Leaf Purple', 'Green Bouquet', and 'Piccolo Fine Verde'.

Lemon basil 'Citriodorum'

Lemon basil 'Citriodorum' has light green leaves and a lemony fragrance. Direct-sow this basil seed so you don't disturb the sensitive roots. The leaves are great in vinegars, potpourri, fruit salad, fish, poultry, and herb teas.

Purple basil

Purple basil has purple foliage and pink flowers. It brings a lot of color to the herb garden and makes a wonderful red herbal vinegar. Some cultivars include 'Purpurascens', much-ruffled 'Purple Ruffles', 'Opal', and dwarf 'Minimum Purpurascens'.

Fragrant basils

Fragrant basils for special kinds of cooking and potpourri include purple-stemmed anise basil, cinnamon basil, and Thai basil.

Thai basil (*O. citriodorum* 'Thai') is an annual native to Thailand and Burma. It has a darker leaf than common basil and a slight anise flavor. It is used extensively in Thai and Indian cooking.

Potential Problems: Japanese beetles can be a pest. Handpick beetles and put them into a container of soapy water and leave overnight to drown.

Harvesting and Using: Cut off the branch tips every few weeks and use the leaves fresh, frozen, or dried with meat, tomatoes, beans, eggs, eggplant, onions, potatoes, salads, cornbread, butters, vinegars, pesto, pasta, or potpourri. Dry the flower heads for wreaths. If you can't use all the basil you harvested right away, place the stems in water on the kitchen counter for a day or two. It doesn't refrigerate well.

Related Herbs: Holy basil (*O. sanctum*) has narrower oval leaves and pink flowers with a perfumed fragrance that's nice in potpourri. It gets to be about 18 inches high.

Basil

Thai Basil

Purple Basil

Bush Basil

Origanum marjorana – Sweet Marjoram

Family: Labiatae

Native of Mediterranean region

Appearance: Tender perennial with sweet-scented, oval gray-green leaves and tiny white flowers in ball-like bracts. Grows a foot high but may flop low to the ground.

Growing Know-How: Plant in well-drained soil and full sun after last frost. Space plants 6 to 8 inches apart. Fertilize with a dilute balanced fertilizer after harvesting to encourage regrowth. Bring healthy plants indoors during winter in cold climates. Pinch back often to keep bushy and prevent seed set.

Propagation: Start seed indoors 6 weeks before last frost. Use sterile growing mix to prevent damping off and sprinkle gently to water. Propagate by division or cuttings.

Potential Problems: None serious.

Harvesting and Using: Cut just before flowering for richest flavor. Harvest as needed for everyday use. The leaves and flower buds are good fresh or dried with chicken, cheese, vegetables, soups, potpourri, and teas.

Related Herbs: Marjoram is part of the oregano genus, which includes many similar herbs. See also Oregano.

Hardy hybrid sweet marjoram (*O. × marjoricum*) is slightly more pungent than sweet marjoram. It is hardy to about 0°F.

Pot marjoram (*O. onites*) is a tender perennial with heart-shaped leaf bases and white or purple flowers. It has a stronger flavor than sweet marjoram.

Dittany of Crete (*O. dictamnus*) is a tender perennial with furry silver leaves on 12-inch-high plants. It has attractive bracts surrounding pink flowers. Because the oregano scent is subdued, you'll enjoy dittany of Crete most as an ornamental container, pot, or rock-garden plant.

Origanum vulgare – Oregano

Family: Labiatae

Native of Mediterranean region

Appearance: Common or wild oregano is a vigorous grower with oval leaves on stems up to 30 inches high. The purple flowers appear in late summer. Some plants have very little flavor and are not used much in cooking. Greek oregano (*O. v.* subsp. *hirtum*), which has a delightful spicy flavor, has furry leaves on stems up to 18 inches high and floppy white flowers.

Growing Know-How: Plant in well-drained soil of moderate fertility and full sun. Space 2 feet apart.

Propagation: Easy to propagate by division or cuttings.

Potential Problems: Provide well-drained soil to prevent root rot. Treat spider mites and aphids with insecticidal soap.

Harvesting and Using: Flowers are attractive dried or fresh. Cut sprigs before flowering or as needed for cooking.

Related Herbs: Wild marjoram or oregano, *O. v.* subsp. *vulgare,* grows 30 inches high with pink flowers that dry well. Other cultivars are 'Dr. Ietswaart', low growing with flavorful golden leaves, 'Compactum Nanum', and 'Golden Creeping'.

Oregano's real relatives include a variety of marjorams and ornamental but not especially flavorful oreganos.

See also Marjoram.

Pelargonium spp. – Scented Geraniums

Family: Geraniaceae

Native of South Africa

Appearance: Rounded to finely cut, furry scented leaves. They can stay as low as 18 inches high or rise up to 3 feet high. The flowers are small and white, purple, or pink.

Growing Know-How: Grow in full sun and well-drained soil of average fertility. You can also grow them in pots outdoors on the patio in summer and indoors in a sunny window or light garden in winter. Fertilize with a balanced organic fertilizer when planting or repotting. Pinch or cut back occasionally to keep the plant bushy. Don't fertilize in winter unless the foliage discolors; then fertilize only lightly.

Cultivars and Related Herbs: There are dozens of different cultivars and species that vary in appearance and fragrance. A few favorites are listed below.

Lemon geranium (*P. crispum*) has a lemon fragrance, tiny lobed leaves with notched edges, and purple flowers. 'Rober's Lemon Rose' (*P. graveolens*) has a rose fragrance, pink flowers, and larger deeply cut leaves. *P. g.* 'Silver Rose' is similar but has gray leaves.

Propagation: Take cuttings in spring or fall to grow over winter indoors. Allow cuttings to sit overnight before putting in moist soil.

Potential Problems: Spray whiteflies with insecticidal soap.

Harvesting and Using: Pick individual leaves for herb wreaths, herb sugars, herb butters, teas, and cakes.

Perilla frutescens – Perilla

Family: Labiatae

Native of Eastern Asia

Appearance: "Beefsteak Plant." Resembles basil. Has cinnamon-mint scented, green or purple foliage, often wrinkled. Grows 3 feet high and bears pink flowers in late summer.

Sweet Marjoram

Scented Geranium

Oregano

Perilla

201

Growing Know-How: Grow in rich but well-drained soil and full sun to light shade. Space plants a foot apart.

Cultivars: 'Crispa' has attractive, extra-crinkled leaves.

Propagation: Sow seeds outdoors in warm soil or indoors 8 weeks before the last spring frost. Seeds need light to sprout.

Potential Problems: Deadhead to prevent invasive self-sowing.

Harvesting and Using: Use as an accent plant. Fresh foliage is used in oriental cuisine; but its safety has been questioned, so consume in moderate quantities.

Petroselinum crispum – Parsley

Family: Umbelliferae
Native of Mediterranean region

Appearance: Deep, carrotlike taproot and flat or frilly leaves 12 to 18 inches high the first year of growth.

Growing Know-How: Plant in rich, moist, but well-drained soil in full sun to light shade 8 to 12 inches apart. Mulch the plants thickly in winter to delay dieback or dig up young plants and bring them indoors to a cool, bright location. During the second year of growth, remove flower stalks to extend the foliage life.

Cultivars: There are three common varieties of parsley: Italian or flat-leaf, curly, and Hamburg.

Italian or flat-leaf parsley (*P. crispum* var. *Neapolitanum*) has flat, dark green leaves with a strong, coarse flavor and edible, succulent stems. Both curly leaf and Italian are used in cooking, but the flavor of the Italian is preferable.

Curly leaf parsley (*P. crispum*) has leaves that curl into small frilly leaflets. It is often used as a garnish and is the variety most commonly sold even though it has less flavor than Italian parsley.

Hamburg parlsey (*P. c.* var. *Tuberosum*) has a thick, celery-flavored root that has a nutty taste when boiled as a vegetable.

Propagation: Grow parsley from seed. Sow outdoors in fall or start the seed indoors 6 to 8 weeks before the last spring frost. Soak seeds in hot water or freeze overnight to speed germination. Transplant while young without disturbing the taproot for best results.

Potential Problems: Aphids can be a problem indoors.

Harvesting and Using: Pinch off parsley sprigs as needed or cut the entire plant back to dry or freeze a larger quantity of foliage. You can munch on it plain for a vitamin-rich snack and breath freshener. Make parsley butter or parsley mayonnaise; use it in almost any dish for mild flavor and rich green color.

Pimpinella anisum – Anise

Family: Umbelliferae
Native of Greece and Egypt

Appearance: A delicate-looking plant that can reach 2 feet in height. Has round to finely cut stem leaves and broader leaves near the ground. In midsummer, the thin stems are topped with umbrella-shaped clusters of white flowers, which are heavy enough to make the stems flop. The seed matures late in the growing season.

Growing Know-How: Give anise well-drained, fertile soil, lots of sun, and a long season of hot weather. Space plants about 6 inches apart so they can lean on each other. At first bloom, apply a balanced organic fertilizer.

Propagation: Start seed in a peat pot in a warm place indoors in late winter or early spring. Transplant seedlings outdoors when the weather gets mild in late spring. Break open the bottom of the pot before planting; be careful not to disturb the taproot.

Potential Problems: None serious.

Harvesting and Using: You can harvest a few leaves to put in salads or make the leaves your main harvest if your season is too short for the seeds to mature. If your plants produce ripe seed, cut off the seed heads and hang them over newspaper in a warm, airy location. The seeds will dry; some will fall on the paper. Remove the remaining seeds and freeze them all for 48 hours to kill any pests or pest eggs. Store in an airtight jar in a cool, dark place. Use the seeds to flavor cookies and breads.

Poterium sanguisorba – Salad Burnet

Family: Rosaceae
Native of Europe

Appearance: Salad burnet starts with a low rosette of dark green, compound leaves that give it a delicate look and make a nice edging. But in late spring, it stretches up 2-foot-high stalks with balls of inconspicuous flowers. Cut them off to keep an edging neat.

Growing Know-How: Plant salad burnet about 12 inches apart in well-drained soil of moderate to low fertility and in full sun. Remove flowers to prevent prolific self-sowing.

Propagation: Sow the seed outdoors in fall or spring or start the seedlings indoors in spring about 6 weeks before the last spring frost. You can also move self-sown seedlings.

Potential Problems: If the soil is not well drained, the roots may rot. Plants die in severe heat.

Harvesting and Using: The leaves stay mild-flavored all season and make a nice addition to salads or vinegars. Dry the flowers for arrangements and wreaths.

Anise Seed

Curly Leaf Parsley

Salad Burnet

Italian Parsley

203

Rosmarinus officinalis – **Rosemary**

Family: Labiatae

Native of Mediterranean region

Appearance: Tender shrub with glossy, strongly scented, ever-green needlelike leaves with a flashy light stripe below and blue, lavender, or white flowers. Flowers are borne on old growth in late winter. When grown outside in warm climates (zones 8–10), most rosemary cultivars can grow up to 6 feet high. Prostrate forms creep along the ground.

Growing Know-How: In warm climates, plant rosemary in well-drained soil and full sun, spacing plants 2 to 3 feet apart. Prune lightly to shape. In cold climates, grow rosemary in pots to bring indoors during winter. Put them in a sunny window or under artifical lights. Use well-drained potting mix and be careful you don't water so much that the soil gets soggy. Fertilize once a month during the growing season with dilute, balanced, organic fertilizer.

Cultivars: In zone 7, try extra-hardy 'Arp' or 'Hill Hardy'. For a bright white flower, grow *R. officinalis* 'Albus'. For baskets or ground covers, try low-growing creeping rosemary, *R. officinalis* 'Prostratus'.

Propagation: Start new plants by layering or stem cuttings. Rosemary will grow from seed, but the process is slow and the seedlings are not true to cultivar.

Potential Problems: Provide well-drained soil to prevent root rot and good air circulation to discourage powdery mildew.

Harvesting and Using: Rosemary has a strong flavor. Use it in bouquet garni with chicken, meat, vegetable, and tomato dishes — pull the leathery sprigs out before serving. You can use rosemary dried or fresh (snip or mince finely).

Rumex scutatus – **French Sorrel**

Family: Polygonaceae

Native of Europe

Appearance: Bright green, arrowhead-shaped leaves that emerge directly from the ground. The leaves can get to be 18 inches high, but the shoots bearing tiny flowers can reach 4 feet high.

Growing Know-How: Plant sorrel in moist, fertile soil, spacing plants 12 inches apart. Fertilize in spring with a balanced organic fertilizer and mulch with compost. Water to keep the soil evenly moist. Cut off flower stems as they emerge, unless you want to use them later for dried flower arrangements. If you do let the seed develop, remove the flower stalks before the seeds can self-sow and become invasive. Uproot excess plants that emerge on runners.

Propagation: You can easily divide existing plants in spring or fall. Or sow seed outdoors in early spring or start it even earlier indoors.

Potential Problems: Catch slugs with beer traps, tubs of beer set in the soil so slugs can crawl in but won't come out.

Harvesting and Using: The tart, lemony-flavored leaves are most tender early in spring but can be good if cooked any time of the growing season. You can steam them with other greens and use them to make sorrel soup or sorrel sauce. The leaves are high in oxalates; avoid them if you're prone to kidney stones.

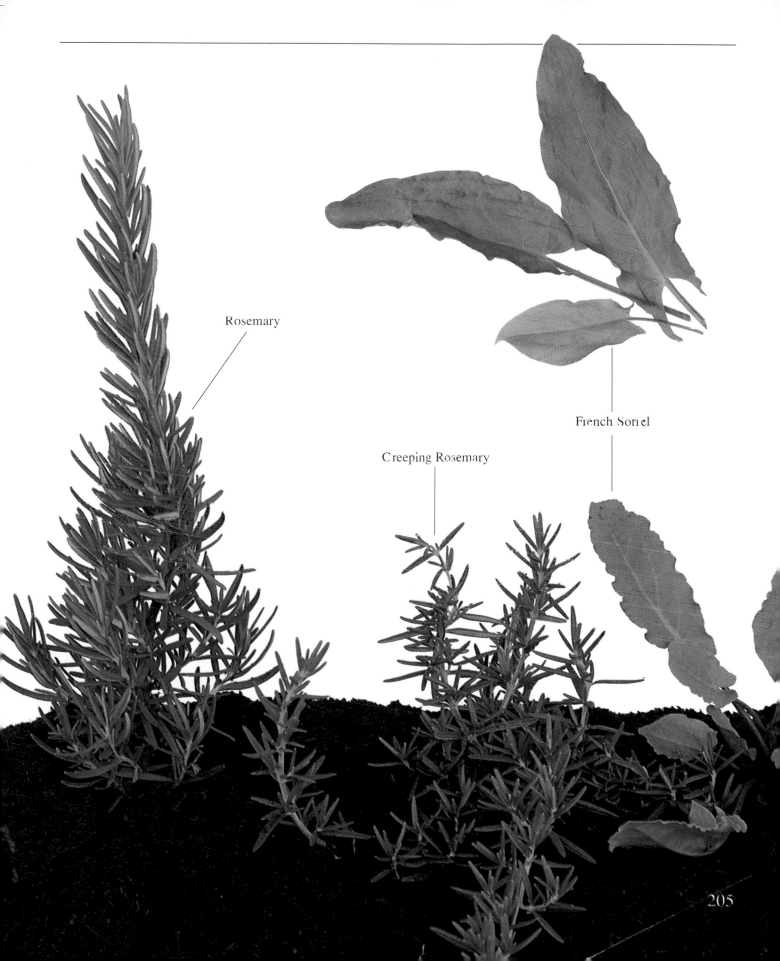

Rosemary

French Sorrel

Creeping Rosemary

Ruta graveolens – Rue

Family: Rutaceae

Native of Southern Europe

Appearance: Handsome blue-tinted leaves held in clusters, plus bright yellow flowers in summer. It reaches about 2 feet high.

Growing Know-How: Rue needs well-drained soil and full sun, although it can survive in light shade. Space plants 18 inches apart. In spring, cut back older stems to encourage new growth.

Cultivars: 'Jackman's Blue' produces no flowers; 'Variegata' has cream or white variegations.

Propagation: You can make more rue plants by dividing the plants in spring, taking root cuttings, or starting seeds indoors about 10 weeks before the last spring frost.

Potential Problems: Provide well-drained soil to prevent root rot.

Harvesting and Using: Rue, once used medicinally, now is primarily a garden ornamental. Avoid touching the leaves, as they make some people break out in a rash.

Salvia officinalis – Sage

Family: Labiatae

Native of Spain to Asia Minor

Appearance: Leathery, gray-green leaves on slightly woody stems up to 2 feet high. The stems don't always support the plant; it can get floppy. It produces attractive spikes of blue-purple (only occasionally white) flowers.

Growing Know-How: Plant sage in well-drained soil and full sun. Space plants 18 to 24 inches apart. Cut back old stems in spring to encourage strong new growth to emerge. Divide every couple of years to rejuvenate plants.

Propagation: You can start the species *Salvia officinalis* from seed fairly easily. Sow the seed indoors 6 to 8 weeks before the last spring frost. You can also divide or take cuttings from existing plants.

Cultivars: You can buy brightly colored, but often less hardy sages. 'Tricolor' has white, rose, and green leaves. 'Purpurea' is a purple-leaved form and 'Icterina' is a golden variegated form. You can also grow dwarf, flop-resistant, silver-leaved sages. Or for a high-performance garden sage, look for 'Berggarten', which has larger-than-average round leaves and a bushy habit that stays full down to the base of the stems.

Potential Problems: Discourage rots and slugs with well-drained soil. Encourage good air circulation to prevent mildew and heat problems.

Harvesting and Using: Sage has the best flavor when used fresh with cheese or chicken dishes and stuffings. Try rubbing a fresh leaf on a pork chop before grilling it. You can also use sage for tea, in limited quantities; it tastes better if mixed with peppermint.

Related Herbs: Clary sage (*S. sclarea*) is a biennial or perennial with beautiful long spikes of white, purple, or blue flowers that can reach 4 feet high. You can use the foliage for potpourri.

S. viridis is an ornamental annual sometimes sold as clary. It produces pink bracts that resemble flowers and make excellent cut or dried flowers, but it has no herbal use.

Purple sage (*S. o.* 'Purpurascens') is a hardy cultivar that grows 18 inches tall. The purple leaves are strongly flavored and can be used in stuffings, omelets, and soups. Purple sage is also planted as an ornamental to complement yellow blossoms in the garden.

Pineapple sage (*S. elegans*) is a perennial in zone 8; it is grown as an annual elsewhere. It has pineapple-scented foliage and spikes of red flowers in late summer and fall. Use its leaves for teas or potpourri, and in fruit salads.

Other related herbs include blue sage (*S. clevelandii*) and silver sage (*S. argentea*).

Purple Sage

Pineapple Sage

Rue

Sage

Santolina chamaecyparissus – Lavender Cotton

Family: Compositae

Native of Mediterranean region

Appearance: This evergreen shrub has neat, fragrant, narrow, and crinkled leaves on mound-shaped plants about 2 feet high. Soft gray leaves give it its name, lavender cotton, also known as gray santolina. Keep the leaves clipped for formal knot gardens, edgings, or clusters, or let the yellow, ball-like flowers emerge for extra color in an informal garden.

Growing Know-How: Like all gray herbs, provide full sun and soil with excellent drainage. In spring, when the new growth emerges, cut off barren stems and cut back healthy stems a little to encourage bushy new growth. In cold climates, mulch with pine boughs during winter.

Propagation: Grow more lavender cotton by layering in the fall or taking cuttings in the spring.

Cultivars: You can find cultivars such as 'Plumosus' with finely cut, feathery-looking leaves.

Potential Problems: Choose a site with good air circulation to prevent rot and death in hot and humid weather.

Harvesting and Using: Make use of the bright foliage for knot gardens, edgings, clumps, and mixed borders. You can cut sprigs for flower arrangements and tussie mussies. You can also use it dried in herb wreaths and potpourri.

Related Herbs: Green santolina *(S. virens)* looks similar to its gray brother but is bright green with a slightly different fragrance and different foliage texture. *S. neapolitana,* rarely sold in the United States, has lacy foliage that's almost white.

Satureja hortensis – Summer Savory

Family: Labiatae

Native of Europe

Appearance: Narrow, dark green, spice-scented leaves on low, bushy plants up to 18 inches high. They are topped with tiny, pale pink flowers in summer.

Growing Know-How: Plant summer savory in well-drained, moderately fertile soil and full sun. Space plants 12 inches apart. To ensure fresh summer savory all season, start a second crop in early summer for late harvests.

Propagation: You can start summer savory from seed, sowing it outdoors in spring. Or start seeds 4 to 6 weeks early indoors.

Potential Problems: Prevent root rot by providing good drainage.

Harvesting and Using: Harvest summer savory as you need it. The rich aroma will be most intense just before the plant flowers. Use it fresh or dried for a pleasant sweet, spicy flavor to beans, vegetables, meats, pastas, and rice. You can also use the leaves in tea.

Related Herbs: Winter savory *(S. montana)* is grown as a perennial in zones 5 to 9. It has foliage similar to summer savory but is spicier and evergreen in mild climates. The plant forms a mat 12 inches high. White flowers appear in late summer. You can propagate winter savory by layering or cuttings. A low-growing form, creeping winter savory *(S. montana* 'Procumbens'), is also available.

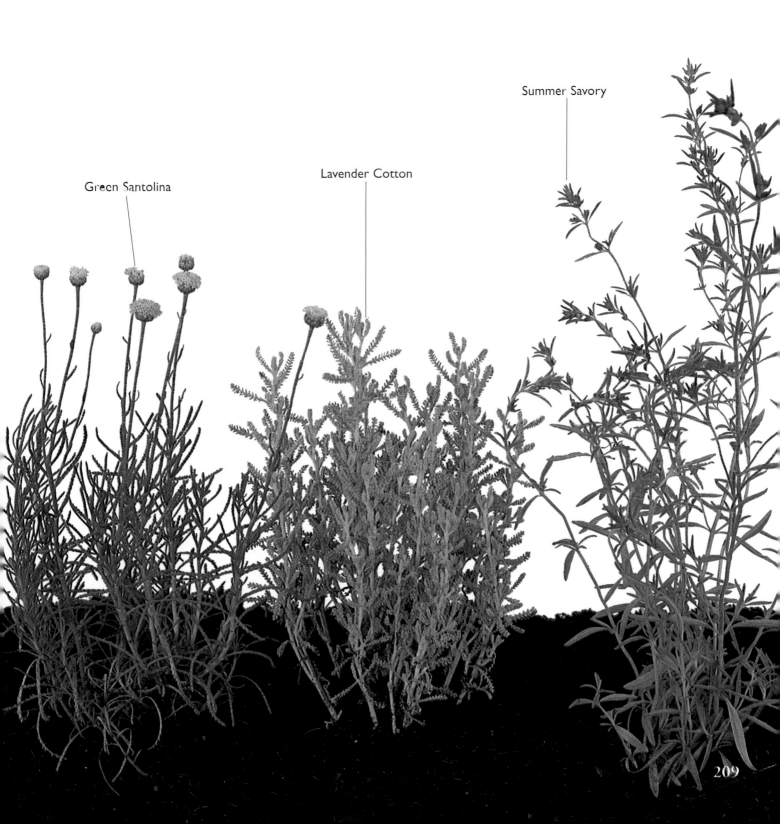

Green Santolina

Lavender Cotton

Summer Savory

Stachys byzantina – Lamb's Ears

Family: Labiatae
Native of Eurasia

Appearance: Lamb's ears grows 6 inches tall with furry, oval leaves that look like their namesake. In spring, the plants send up furry silver stalks of pink flower spikes to about 2 feet high.

Growing Know-How: Plant about 12 to 18 inches apart in well-drained, moderately fertile soil in a sunny site. Trim back in spring, and be sure to groom frequently to remove old or dead leaves. The plant can spread moderately quickly, so be prepared to divide as necessary.

Cultivars: 'Silver Carpet' produces no flowers. 'Helen Von Stein' (pictured at right) has large leaves (the cultivar is also called 'Big Ears') and especially attractive foliage.

Propagation: Propagate by division.

Potential Problems: In wet soils, the plant may suffer root and crown rot. It can't take hot humid weather — it rots.

Harvesting and Using: Use the plant as a silver-leaved ornamental. Cut the flowers to dry and use in wreaths and arrangements.

Related Herbs: Betony (*S. officinalis*) is an old-fashioned medicinal plant with attractive oval leaves that are smooth to densely hairy. In summer, betony sends up spikes of pale magenta (occasionally pink or white) flowers up to 3 feet high.

Cultivars of betony include 'Alba', which produces white flowers, and 'Grandiflora', which is characterized by large, soft, pink flowers.

Symphytum officinale – Comfrey

Family: Boraginaceae
Native of Russia

Appearance: Long, hairy lower leaves and upright clusters of white, pink, purple, or yellow flowers that can reach 3 feet high.

Growing Know-How: Give comfrey moist, loose soil in full sun. Space plants about 3½ feet apart.

Propagation: Sow comfrey seed outdoors in fall or spring. You can also transplant divisions of existing plants. Pieces of the root will often sprout, so once planted, comfrey is very hard to eradicate. It can also spread to invade adjacent plantings.

Cultivars: Handsome variegated forms have white-edged leaves.

Potential Problems: To avoid Japanese beetles, trap them with pheromone lures in a far corner of the yard and treat your lawn with milky spore disease. Or handpick and drop them into a container of soapy water.

Harvesting and Using: Comfrey has long been made into medicinal teas, but its safety for human use is now questioned.

Related Herbs: Caucasian comfrey (*S. caucasicum*) has handsome pink buds that open to reveal blue or white flowers. Some forms have leaf variegation, too. It grows 2 feet high.

Russian comfrey (*S. x uplandicum*) has pink buds that open to reveal purple flowers. It reaches 6 feet high.

Tagetes lucida – Mexican Mint Marigold

Family: Compositae
Native of Mexico

Appearance: An unusual 30-inch-high marigold grown for its licorice-flavored leaves. As a bonus, you'll get pretty but small yellow flowers in fall.

Growing Know-How: Mexican mint marigold thrives in hot weather and needs a long, warm growing season to be most productive. Plant it in well-drained soil and full sun after the last spring frost. Space plants 12 inches apart. Pinch occasionally for bushier plants. In cold climates, you can bring the plants indoors to a warm, bright location in winter.

Propagation: In cold climates, start the seeds indoors 6 weeks before the last spring frost. You can also start new plants from cuttings.

Potential Problems: None serious.

Harvesting and Using: Harvest individual leaves or sprigs as needed. Use them in any dish calling for tarragon or other anise-flavored herbs, or in teas and potpourri.

Related Herbs: Signet marigolds (*T. tenuifolia*) include citrus-scented 'Lemon Gem' and 'Orange Gem' cultivars. They have delicate, fragrant leaves and small yellow or orange flowers.

Comfrey

Mexican Mint Marigold

Lamb's Ears

Teucrium chamaedrys – Germander

Family: Labiatae
Native of Eurasia

Appearance: Best known for its handsome, notched, evergreen leaves, which you can prune into a neat mound or edging. If you don't shear the plant, it will produce pink flower spikes in late summer. The foliage grows about 12 inches high, although you can keep it pruned shorter, and the flowers stretch up to about 18 inches high.

Growing Know-How: Grow germander in full sun and well-drained soil of moderate fertility. Keep it out of the wind to prevent damage to the evergreen foliage and cover with pine boughs during winter. Remove dead or damaged growth in spring. You can shear germander regularly to maintain a desired shape, but stop in late summer in climates with cold winters.

Propagation: You can start germander quickly from root divisions and stem cuttings or slowly from seed.

Cultivars: Prostrate germander (*T. chamaedrys* 'Prostratum') is a vigorous creeping plant that only reaches 10 inches high.

Variegated germander is a full-sized germander with yellow and white variegations.

Potential Problems: None serious.

Harvesting and Using: Use germander as an herb garden ornamental. Historically it was used for medicinal purposes.

Related Herbs: *T. flavum,* a marginally hardy germander, has large, sometimes furry leaves with yellow flowers on plants about 2 feet tall.

Caucasian germander *(T. hircanicum)* is a hardy perennial with furry leaves and purple or red flowers on plants that are 2 feet tall.

Thymus vulgaris – Common Thyme

Family: Labiatae
Native of Mediterranean region

Appearance: Small, glossy green leaves clustered along slender woody stems and charming clusters of white or pink flowers in summer. It grows to 12 inches high. It's an excellent edger or front-of-the-border plant.

Growing Know-How: Plant thyme in well-drained, sandy soil and full sun. Thyme also grows well in containers. Space plants 12 to 18 inches apart. Cut the woody stems back by about half in spring to encourage healthy new growth. Divide clumps every couple of years to keep them tidy and vigorous.

Propagation: The easiest way to propagate thyme is to divide it in spring. You can also root stem cuttings.

Cultivars: Cultivars of this species include 'Broadleaf English' and 'Variegated English'.

Potential Problems: If your thyme has problems with fungus, thin out thick-growing mats to encourage better air circulation. Provide very good drainage to discourage root rot.

Harvesting and Using: Harvest thyme sprigs just before bloom for maximum flavor. You can also harvest earlier and later in the season, but stop harvesting in late summer to discourage winter damage. Use thyme when cooking meat, potatoes, soups, creamed dishes, stuffings, and for teas and wreaths.

Related Herbs: Caraway thyme (*T. Herba-barona*) is a rapidly spreading, low-growing herb with a distinctive aroma. Mother-of-thyme or wild thyme is *T. pulegioides,* which includes cultivars such as 'Fosterflower', 'Gold Dust', and 'Oregano-Scented'. Other Mother-of-thyme cultivars are 'Annie Hall', 'Coccineus', 'Hall's Woolly', and 'White Moss'.

Golden lemon thyme (*T. × citriodorus*) is a low, spreading shrub. Golden yellow leaves are small and oval and quite fragrant when crushed.

Tropaeolum majus – Nasturtium

Family: Tropaeolaceae
Native of South America

Appearance: Nasturtium has interesting round, watercress-flavored leaves and complex-shaped red, yellow, or orange flowers on bushy or vining plants. Flowers are as attractive as they are good to eat.

Growing Know-How: Plant nasturtiums in well-drained soil and full sun, or light shade in hot climates. Space seeds of bushy cultivars about 8 inches apart; space vining cultivars 18 inches apart. Fertilize with a balanced organic fertilizer in spring to encourage more flower development.

Propagation: Sow seed outdoors after the last spring frost.

Cultivars: You can find an assortment of different flower colors and shapes, also cultivars with variegated foliage.

Potential Problems: Spray aphids with insecticidal soap.

Growing and Using: Harvest the peppery leaves and flowers for salads, vinegars, and cheese sandwiches. The flowers make a colorful herb vinegar. You can pickle the seeds and use them as you would capers.

Germander

Thyme

Nasturtium

213

APPENDICES

Mail-Order Nurseries & Herb Suppliers

Brown's Edgewood Gardens
2611 Corrine Drive
Orlando, FL 32803
407-896-3203

Companion Plants
7247 N. Codville Ridge Road
Athens, OH 45701
614-592-4643

The Cook's Garden
P.O. Box 535
Londonderry, VT 05148
800-457-9703

The Daffodil Mart
7463 Heath Trail
Gloucester, VA 23061
800-255-2852

T. DeBaggio Herbs
923 N. Ivy Street
Arlington, VA 22201
703-243-2498

Filaree Farm
182 Conconully Highway
Okanogan, WA 98840-9774
509-422-6940

Gardener's Supply Retail Store
128 Intervale Road
Burlington, VT 05401
800-955-3370

Gardens Alive!
(organic gardening products)
5100 Schenley Place
Lawrenceburg, IN 47025
812-537-8677

The Gourmet Garden
8650 College Boulevard
Overland Park, KS 66210
913-451-2443

Legacy Herbs
HC 70, Box 442
Mountain View, AR 72560
501-269-4051

Lily of the Valley Herb Farm
3969 Fox Avenue
Minerva, OH 44657
330-862-3920

Logee's Greenhouses
141 North Street
Danielson, CT 06239
888-330-8038

The Natural Gardening Company
217 San Anselmo Avenue
San Anselmo, CA 94960
707-766-9303

Nichols Garden Nursery
1190 North Pacific Way
Albany, OR 97321-4598
541-928-9280

George W. Park Seed Company
Box 31
Cokesbury Road (Hwy. 254 N.)
Greenwood, SC 29647-000
800-845-3369

Peaceful Valley Farm Supply
110 Spring Hill Drive #2
P.O. Box 2209
Grass Valley, CA 95945
530-272-4769

Rabbit Shadow Farm
2880 E. Hwy. 402
Loveland, CO 80537
800-850-5531

Redwood City Seed Company
P.O. Box 361
Redwood City, CA 94064
650-325-7333

Shepherd's Garden Seeds
30 Irene Street
Torrington, CT 06790
860-482-3638

Sunnybrook Farms Nursery
9448 Mayfield Road
Chesterland, OH 44026
440-729-7232

In addition to contacting the above sources, consider contacting other herb gardeners by checking your local newspaper for listings of group meetings or special events. Club meetings, herb fairs, and herb sales or herb-related groups may be listed there.

Look in your telephone book yellow pages under nurseries or greenhouses for growers specializing in herbs. Talk to them about what's happening in the herb scene locally.

Contact your Cooperative Extension Service horticultural or agricultural agents, who should be listed in the yellow pages under county offices. They may know people who are studying herbs.

Get in touch with the national offices of the Herb Society of America to see if any groups near you are welcoming new members or to join at-large. Write to HSA, 9019 Kirtland Chardon Road, Kirtland, OH 44094.

If you're interested in growing herbs as a business, contact the Herb Growing and Marketing Network (publishers of the *Herbal Connection* and the *Herbal Green Pages),* P.O. Box 245, Silver Spring, PA 17575-0245, or the International Herb Association, 1202 Allanson Road, Mundelein, IL 60060.

If you want to stay up-to-date with current developments in the herb field, subscribe to *HerbalGram,* published by the American Botanical Council, which offers a variety of other research and educational programs; write to P.O. Box 201660, Austin, TX 78720. *HerbalGram* is also published by the Herb Research Foundation, a research center that welcomes members; write to 1007 Pearl Street, Suite 200, Boulder, CO 80302.

Sources

Herb Research Foundation (1007 Pearl St., Boulder, CO 80302) is a non-profit organization with a library of resources devoted to herbs. Call 303-449-2265 for more information on how to join.

NAPRALERT (University of Chicago) is a computer database of information on herbs providing citations and article summaries from over 100,000 references — ancient herbals to modern scientific journals. You can access NAPRALERT with your computer modem through BIT-NET, Internet, CompuServe, and Prodigy. For more information, call 312-996-2246.

Acknowledgments

The following individuals were very gracious in granting me personal interviews that, for the most part, were held over the phone as I researched for this book. For their generous time and patient explanations, I thank the following:

Millie Adams

Dan Banks

Jim Becker

Jolie Bishop

Margaret Blank

Mark Blumenthal

Peter Borchard

Miram Bowden

Libby Bruch

Tom DeBaggio

Huck DeVenzio

Ron Engleman

Norman Farnsworth

Mark Fenton

Steven Foster

Lane Furneaux

Rolfe Hagen

Charles Hall

Tom Harrison

Madelene Hill

Brian Holley

Jerry Hood

Tovah Martin

Rose Marie Nichols
  McGee

Kellie O'Brien

Maureen Rogers

Ruthie Ryden

Caryl Saunders

Cathy Sebastian

Glenna Sheaffer

Renée Shepherd

Moshe Shiffrne

Holly Shimizu

Marty Sickinger

Diane Morey Sitton

Karen Small

Tony Spicer

Cyndi Spresser

Thea Steinmetz

Bob Surbella

Arthur Tucker

Ruth Weisheit

Experts Cited

Millie Adams is a home economist, gardener, and expert cook in Columbus, Ohio.

Jim Becker owns and operates Goodwin Creek Garden, a mail-order nursery of herb and flower plants and seeds in Williams, Oregon. Jim and his wife, Dotti, are authors of *An Everlasting Garden* (Interweave Press).

Mark Blumenthal is the president and founder of the American Botanical Council in Austin, Texas. He edits and publishes *HerbalGram,* an international quarterly devoted to subjects of interest to the herb trade.

Peter Borchard is owner of Companion Plants, a nursery and seed house with an extensive listing of about 600 herbs and companion plants in Athens, Ohio. Although the nursery is most involved in mail-order trade, Borchard keeps it open to the public and maintains several acres of display gardens and seed beds.

Libby Bruch, who was kind enough to review this book in manuscript form — and who gave me valuable feedback — owns and operates Quailcrest Farm, a nursery with a wide selection of herbs and charming herb gardens in Wooster, Ohio.

Tom DeBaggio is owner and operator of T. DeBaggio Herbs in Arlington, Virginia. He has introduced a number of new herb plants and developed special production methods of note. He is also a writer and editor, contributing regularly to *the Herb Companion* and other magazines, and has authored *Growing Herbs from Seed, Cutting, and Root: An adventure in small miracles* (Interweave Press).

Ron Engleman is an Oregon-based garlic grower and author of *Growing Great Garlic* (Filaree Productions). He has devised a popular system for organizing different kinds of garlic, most of which he offers in his extensive mail-order cataogue.

Steven Foster, author, photographer, and consultant in medicinal and aromatic plants from Fayetteville, Arkansas, is well known in herbal circles. His most recent book is *Herbal Renaissance* (Gibbs Smith Publisher), and he has also written a variety of other books including *A Field Guide to Medicinal Plants* (Houghton Mifflin's Peterson Series).

Rolfe Hagen is co-owner of the Thyme Garden in Alsea, Oregon. The Thyme Garden is nestled in the coastal range mountains, surrounded by a wonderful wild landscape and herb garden that let customers experience the look and aromas of mature herbs. Rolfe and his wife, Janet, got interested in herbs when they owned a restaurant that featured herbal cuisine.

Madelene Hill is a well-known author, lecturer, and former president of the Herb Society of America who has devoted her entire life to studying herbs. She has developed many trend-setting methods for using herbs and written about them with her daughter, Gwen Barclay, in their book, *Southern Herb Growing* (Shearer Publications, 1987). Hill was formerly a nurseryman at Hilltop Herb Farm in Texas; she and Gwen are now affiliated with Festival Hill Institute, a center for performing arts.

Brian Holley is author, lecturer, and executive director of Cleveland Botanical Garden and former horticulturist, manager of marketing and communications, and supervisor of the teaching garden for the Royal Botanical Gardens, Ontario.

Kellie O'Brien is a popular designer with the Hinsdale, Illinois, firm, English Gardens, Ltd. Her work has been featured in home and garden magazines.

Renée Shepherd owns and operates Shepherd's Garden Seeds, mail-order seed house with trial gardens, test kitchens, and several excellent recipe books, a series called *Recipes from a Kitchen Garden.*

Holly Shimizu is assistant executive director of the U.S. Botanic Garden and former curator of the National Herb Garden at the U.S. National Arboretum.

Diane Morey Sitton is an avid herb grower and author of the *Texas Gardener's Guide to Growing and Using Herbs.* She lives in Colmesneil, Texas.

Karen Small and Cyndi Spresser are cooks and owners of Jezebel's, an innovative small restaurant open for breakfast and lunch in Chagrin Falls, Ohio.

Arthur Tucker is a research scientist for the Department of Agriculture and Natural Resources at Delaware State College in Dover, Delaware. He has made great strides in untangling herb nomenclature and clearing up the identities of mislabeled herbs.

Jim Wilson is the former host of the Victory Garden television show and a former herb grower in Donalds, South Carolina. He is author of *Landscaping with Herbs* (Houghton Mifflin) and a number of other books.

Laurie Zaim is an innovative cook who likes to grow her own herbs. She lives in Chagrin Falls, Ohio.

Spring and Fall Frost Dates in Canada

Station	Last Frost	First Frost	Station	Last Frost	First Frost
British Columbia			**Ontario** — *continued*		
Chilliwack	Apr. 6	Nov. 9	Owen Sound	May 12	Oct. 15
Dawson Creek	June 5	Aug. 29	Parry Sound	May 17	Sept. 28
Kamloops	May 1	Oct. 5	Peterborough	May 18	Sept. 20
Kelowna	May 19	Sept. 20	St. Catharines	May 2	Oct. 17
Nanaimo	Apr. 28	Oct. 17	Sudbury	May 17	Sept. 25
Port Alberni	May 8	Oct. 15	Thunder Bay	June 1	Sept. 15
Prince George	June 4	Sept. 3	Timmins	June 8	Sept. 6
Terrace	May 5	Oct. 17	Toronto	May 9	Oct. 6
Vancouver	Mar. 28	Nov. 5	Windsor	Apr. 25	Oct. 22
Vernon	Apr. 29	Oct. 4			
Victoria	Apr. 19	Nov. 5	**Quebec**		
			Baie Comeau	May 28	Sept. 15
Northwest Territory and Yukon			Chicoutimi	May 17	Sept. 30
Whitehorse	June 11	Aug. 25	Montreal	May 3	Oct. 7
Yellowknife	May 27	Sept. 15	Quebec	May 13	Sept. 29
			Rimouski	May 13	Sept. 30
Alberta			Sherbrooke	June 1	Sept. 10
Athabaska	June 1	Aug. 29	Trois-Rivieres	May 19	Sept. 23
Calgary	May 23	Sept. 15	Thetford Mines	May 28	Sept. 14
Edmonton	May 7	Sept. 23			
Grande Prairie	May 18	Sept. 13	**New Brunswick**		
Lethbridge	May 17	Sept. 18	Bathurst	May 19	Sept. 26
Medicine Hat	May 16	Sept. 22	Edmundston	May 28	Sept. 18
Red Deer	May 25	Sept. 9	Fredericton	May 20	Sept. 22
			Grand Falls	May 24	Sept. 24
Saskatchewan			Moncton	May 24	Sept. 27
Moose Jaw	May 20	Sept. 18	Saint John	May 18	Oct. 4
Prince Albert	June 2	Sept. 4			
Regina	May 21	Sept. 10	**Prince Edward Island**		
Saskatoon	May 21	Sept. 15	Charlottetown	May 17	Oct. 14
Weyburn	May 22	Sept. 12	Summerside	May 9	Oct. 19
			Tignish	May 23	Oct. 9
Manitoba					
Brandon	May 27	Sept. 10	**Nova Scotia**		
The Pas	May 27	Sept. 17	Halifax	May 6	Oct. 20
Thompson	June 15	Aug. 16	Kentville	May 16	Oct. 5
Winnipeg	May 25	Sept. 22	Shelburne	May 14	Sept. 29
			Sydney	May 24	Oct. 13
Ontario			Yarmouth	May 1	Oct. 18
Barrie	May 26	Sept. 16			
Hamilton	Apr. 29	Oct. 15	**Newfoundland**		
Kingston	May 2	Oct. 10	Corner Brook	May 22	Oct. 12
London	May 9	Oct. 8	Grand Falls	June 2	Sept. 26
Ottawa	May 6	Oct. 5	St. John's	June 2	Oct. 12

Data from Environmental Canada as published in *Canadian Gardening* magazine.

NO POSTAGE
NECESSARY
IF MAILED
IN THE
UNITED STATES

BUSINESS REPLY MAIL
FIRST-CLASS MAIL PERMIT NO. 2 POWNAL VT

POSTAGE WILL BE PAID BY ADDRESSEE

STOREY'S BOOKS FOR COUNTRY LIVING
STOREY COMMUNICATIONS INC
RR1 BOX 105
POWNAL VT 05261-9988

From:

Herbal Renaissance.
ty, UT: Gibbs Smith

an. *The Heirloom
cting & Growing over
hioned Ornamentals.*
Storey/Garden Way
1992.

*Herbs for the Holidays:
Decorations.* Pownal,
Garden Way Publishing,

ra. *Green Pharmacy.*
T: Healing Arts Press,

semary. *A Gift Book of
al, VT: Storey
1994.

. *The Moosewood
Restaurant Kitchen Garden.* New
York: Fireside Books, 1992.

Duff, Gail. *Natural Fragrances,
Outdoor Scents for Indoor Uses.*
Pownal, VT: Storey/Garden Way
Publishing, 1989.

Duke, James A. *Handbook of Edible
Weeds.* Boca Raton, FL: CRC
Press, 1992.

Engleman, Ron. *Growing Great
Garlic.* Okanogan, WA: Filaree
Productions, 1995.

Forsell, Mary. *Heirloom Herbs.* New
York: Villard Books, 1991.

Foster, Steven. *Herbal Emissaries.*
Rochester, VT: Healing Arts Press,
1992.

Jacobs, Betty E.M. *Growing & Using
Herbs Successfully.* Pownal, VT:
Storey/Garden Way Publishing,
1981.

Mabey, Richard. *The New Age
Herbalist.* New York: Macmillan,
1988.

Marcin, Marietta Marshall. *The
Herbal Tea Garden: Planning,
Planting, Harvesting & Brewing.*
Pownal, VT: Storey/Garden Way
Publishing, 1993.

Michalak, Patricia. *Rodale's Successful Organic Gardening Herbs.* Emmaus, PA: Rodale Press, 1993.

Newdick, Jane. *At Home with Herbs: Inspiring Ideas for Cooking, Crafts, Decorating, and Cosmetics.* Pownal, VT: Storey Publishing, 1994.

Norris, Dorry Baird. *Sage Cottage Herb Garden Cookbook.* Chester, CT: Globe Pequot Press, 1995.

Oster, Maggie. *Herbal Vinegar.* Pownal, VT: Storey Publishing, 1994.

Pennington, Jean. *Food Values.* New York: Harper and Row, 1989.

Powell, Eileen. *From Seed to Bloom: How to Grow over 500 Annuals, Perennials & Herbs.* Pownal, VT: Storey/Garden Way Publishing, 1995.

Reilly, Ann, and Susan Roth. *The Home Landscaper.* Tucson, AZ: Home Planners, 1990.

Reppert, Bertha. *Growing Your Herb Business.* Pownal, VT: Storey Publishing, 1994.

Reppert, Bertha. *Herbs for Weddings and Other Celebrations: A Treasury of Recipes, Gifts & Decorations.* Pownal, VT: Storey/Garden Way Publishing, 1993.

Rohde, Eleanour Sinclair. *A Garden of Herbs.* Boston: Hale, Cushman, and Flint, 1969.

Shaudys, Phyllis V. *Herbal Treasures: Inspiring Month-by-Month Projects for Gardening, Cooking, and Crafts.* Pownal, VT: Storey/Garden Way Publishing, 1990.

Shaudys, Phyllis. *The Pleasure of Herbs: A Month-by-Month Guide to Growing, Using, and Enjoying Herbs.* Pownal, VT: Storey/Garden Way Publishing, 1986.

Simmons, Adelma Grenier. *Herb Gardening in Five Seasons.* New York: Hawthorn Books, 1964.

Tourles, Stephanie L. *The Herbal Body Book.* Pownal, VT: Storey Publishing, 1994.

U.S. Dept. of Agriculture Research Service. *Composition of Foods.* Agriculture Handbook No. 8.2, 1977.

INDEX

Page references in *italic* indicate illustrations;
those in **bold** indicate charts.

D